BOSTON
SPORTS FIRSTS

OWEN FINNEGAN

Commonwealth Editions
Beverly, Massachusetts

To my wife, Nancy; my children, Amy and O.J.; my mother, Rosa;
and my mother-in-law, Irene—for your support and encouragement

ISBN-13: 978-1-933212-50-0
ISBN-10: 1-933212-50-0

Cover, interior design, and illustrations by John Barnett/4 Eyes Design
Printed in the United States of America

Commonwealth Editions is an imprint of Memoirs Unlimited, Inc.,
266 Cabot Street, Beverly, Massachusetts 01915.
Visit us on the Web at www.commonwealtheditions.com.

CONTENTS

BOSTON RED SOX

1. Which Red Sox star was one of the first two Major League players to compete in both the Rose Bowl and the World Series?

2. Which one-time Red Sox pitcher was the first reliever to save at least 40 games in four seasons?

3. Which one-time Red Sox pitcher appeared on a *Sports Illustrated* cover with *Sesame Street's* "Big Bird"?

4. Which Red Sox pitcher gave up a 61st home run of the season to a Major League hitter?

5. Which Red Sox pitcher between 1993 and 2006 threw more than 170 pitches in a game?

6. Which two Red Sox outfielders' first three Major League hits were home runs?

7. Which one-time Red Sox pitcher and Hall of Famer is credited with being the first to use the term "walk-off home run"?

8. Which two Red Sox pitchers recorded six wins in September?

9. Who was the first Red Sox rookie to hit 20 home runs and steal 20 bases?

10. Which one-time Red Sox player was the first pitcher to win an All-Star game, a League Championship Series game, and a World Series game?

11. Can you name the Red Sox player who was elected to two positions in the same All-Star game?

12. Which Red Sox player was the first ever to pinch-hit home runs in both games of a doubleheader?

13. Which Red Sox player hit over .300 in a season while having more walks than hits?

14. Which Red Sox player was the first in baseball history to hit three home runs in a span of two innings?

15. Who was the first Red Sox pitcher to start five consecutive home openers?

16. Which three Red Sox pitchers led the American League in saves for a season?

17. Can you name the Red Sox Hall of Famer who was the first American League hitter to face three different pitchers in an inning?

18. Who was the first Red Sox player ever to hit into a triple play and hit a grand slam in the same game?

19. Which Red Sox player was the first American League hitter with two three-home-run games in the same season?

20. Can you name the first Red Sox hitter to hit three home runs in consecutive at-bats?

21. Who are the first three pitchers to throw at least 2,000 innings for the Red Sox? (Two were still active in 2006.)

22. Who was the first Red Sox pitcher to steal home?

23. Which Red Sox player hit 40 or more doubles in seven consecutive seasons?

24. Who was the first Red Sox player to win a batting title but drive in fewer than 40 runs in the same season?

25. Which Red Sox player appeared in a Little League World Series, a College World Series, and a Major League World Series?

26. Which Red Sox pitcher appeared in 70 or more games three years in a row?

27. Which two Red Sox players had back-to-back seasons of 40 home runs or more?

28. Can you name the Red Sox reliever who recorded 18 consecutive saves to start a season?

29. Who are the two Red Sox players who successfully accomplished the "hidden ball trick" three times in their careers?

30. Which left-handed Red Sox hitter had more than 670 at bats in a season?

31. Who were the first two Red Sox rookie pitchers to make All-Star teams?

32. Which Red Sox player is first (as of 2006) in team career intentional walks?

33. Can you name the Red Sox player who had 30 home runs at an All-Star break?

34. Mark Loretta was the first Red Sox All-Star at second base since what player in the 1960s?

35. In 2006, David Ortiz and Mark Loretta were the first All-Star combo for the Red Sox right side since which two players in the 1950s?

36. Which Red Sox outfielder was first to employ the sliding catch popular in the field today and was the first Red Sox to play on four World Series champions?

37. Two of the three players to collect 200 hits in a season in each league are Steve Sax and Al Oliver. Which Red Sox player was the third?

38. Which one-time Red Sox player was the first infielder to become a member of the "30/30 Club" (30 home runs and 30 steals in the same season)?

39. Can you name the Red Sox player who was first to win a batting title while playing five different positions?

40. The opening game of the 1918 World Series between the Red Sox and Chicago started what tradition at sporting events?

41. Which Red Sox player was first in the American League to score six runs in one game?

42. Which Sox player was the first in Red Sox history to leave 12 men on base in a single game?

43. Who was the first Red Sox player to have his photo featured on a famous TV sitcom?

44. Can you name the Red Sox player who was paid tribute in every episode of a famous TV police drama?

45. What unique Red Sox item was carried to the top of Mount Everest?

46. Who was the Red Sox player said to be the first to cover his mouth with his glove during mound conferences?

47. Who was the first Red Sox reliever to work enough innings in a season to qualify for the ERA title?

48. Can you name the first Red Sox player whom fans voted an All-Star starter at two different infield positions in the same season?

49. Which 2006 Red Sox player was the first in Major League history to have six seasons with six or more home runs in less than 200 at bats?

50. After Carlton Fisk's 1980 departure from the Red Sox, can you name the first three players to come out of the Sox system and become number-one catchers for the team?

51. Can you name the 2006 Red Sox teammates, the first in at least 40 years, to double three times each in the same game?

52. Which one-time Red Sox player, active with another team in 2006, was a first-team high school All-Star basketball player in Michigan with NBA star Chris Webber?

53. In 1986 what Red Sox player became the first Major Leaguer in 40 years to score six runs in a game?

54. In 2002, when Joe Kerrigan was fired as Red Sox manager, who was named interim manager before the hiring of Grady Little as full-time manager?

55. In 1992 what pitcher became the third pitcher in baseball history, and first Red Sox pitcher ever, to pitch a complete-game no-hitter and lose?

56. In 1965 which Red Sox player pinch-hit home runs in back-to-back games, tying a Major League record?

57. In a 1934 exhibition game which Olympic star pitched an inning against the Red Sox?

58. Which two future Hall of Famers were released in 1973 by the Red Sox?

59. Which Red Sox player was a candidate for president on the "Rhinoceros Party" ticket?

60. Who was the Red Sox rookie to receive 13 intentional walks in his rookie year?

61. Who was the Red Sox player who claimed that he had willed himself invisible to escape a knife-wielding attacker?

62. Which Red Sox pitcher was the first starting pitcher to give up 16 hits in a game?

63. Who was the first Red Sox player to hit three bases-loaded triples in a season, equaling a Major League record?

64. Which famous Red Sox player said he was tired of baseball and wanted to be a fireman in New York like his uncle?

65. Who was the first Red Sox opponent to hit three home runs in a game at Fenway Park?

66. Which two opposing players had the most career home runs against the Red Sox as of 2006?

67. Who was the first Red Sox opponent to be named after a Boston Bruins hockey star?

68. Which two Red Sox rookies share the Major League record for hitting two grand slams in their rookie seasons?

69. Can you name the one-time Red Sox player who is among the first four Major League players with 50 home runs and 200 hits in a season?

70. Which Red Sox player said he didn't believe in dinosaurs because he had never seen one?

71. Who was the only left-hander to start a game for the Red Sox in 2004?

72. Which two Red Sox players held record-release parties?

73. Which recent Red Sox third base coach had six base runners cut down in a 12-day period?

74. Who was the first 17-year-old to play for the Red Sox?

75. Who was the first Red Sox player to hit home runs in five consecutive games?

76. Can you name the Red Sox player who was first to have 100 or more hits in each of his first 20 seasons?

77. Who was the first Red Sox player to lead the league in both hits and bases on balls in one season?

78. Which Red Sox player had a Boeing 757 named after him?

79. Who was the first Red Sox pitcher to deliver a pitch in the World Series?

80. Can you name the hearing-impaired player who homered for the Red Sox in his very first plate appearance?

81. A Red Sox player is one of two players who had three consecutive seasons of 200 hits and 100 walks. Who is he?

82. Who was the first Red Sox catcher to both score and drive in 100 runs in a season?

83. Which Red Sox pitcher was the first native of Canada to start a World Series game?

84. Which Red Sox player was first to be awarded a monetary settlement for the misdiagnosis of an injury by the team?

85. Name the first Red Sox pitcher to have 17 postseason appearances with the team.

86. Which Red Sox manager was a one-time snowplow driver on the Massachusetts Turnpike during off-seasons?

87. Which Red Sox pitcher was arrested and charged with attempted murder?

88. Which pitcher acquired by the Red Sox in 1973 was first among active pitchers in career Major League wins at the time?

89. Which one-time Red Sox pitcher was (until 2004) first alphabetically in a list of all-time Major League pitchers?

90. Which Red Sox pitcher was first to have a 3-0 World Series record for the team?

91. Who was the only Red Sox outfielder between 1970 and 2006 to record three assists in a game?

92. Which one-time Red Sox player was the first hitter to hit three grand slams in one month?

93. Can you name the one-time Red Sox player who was the first right-handed hitter to hit 58 home runs in a season?

94. Which former Red Sox player was first to hit a home run in 33 Major League parks?

95. Which person associated with the Red Sox was the first man posthumously inducted into the Baseball Hall of Fame?

96. Which early Red Sox star was the first player to lead off both games of a doubleheader with a home run?

97. Name the Red Sox player who was the first in baseball history to make the final out in a World Series and join his World Series opponent the following season.

98. Which former Red Sox player became the first manager of the Colorado Rockies?

99. Name the first two Red Sox pitchers to record a 5-0 record in April.

100. Who was the first Red Sox player since Ted Williams in 1947 to lead the league in home runs and RBIs and still not win the MVP?

101. Can you name the one-time Red Sox manager who was the first manager to win at least 100 games with six different teams?

102. Which Red Sox player was the first to drive in at least 100 runs but score fewer than 50 runs in the same season?

103. Which one-time Red Sox player was the first to win the MVP award with more than 200 at bats as a designated hitter?

104. Which Red Sox pitcher, while with another team, was one of two teammates to strike out 300-plus hitters in the same season?

105. Which Red Sox player was the first Major Leaguer to hit two home runs in a World Series game?

106. Can you name the one-time Red Sox player who was the first non-U.S. native to reach 400 career home runs?

107. In 2002 this Red Sox pitcher became the first to throw a no-hitter after a 40-save season. Who was he?

108. Which Red Sox employee was the first female public-address announcer in Major League baseball?

109. Which Red Sox pitcher was the first African-American to throw an American League no-hitter?

110. Who was the first Red Sox second baseman to win a Gold Glove?

111. Which Red Sox great was the first player to have part of the playing field named after him?

112. Who was the first Red Sox player to wear uniform #13?

113. On September 24, 1940, the Red Sox became the first team to hit four home runs in an inning. Three of the four players were Hall of Famers. Can you name them?

114. In 2002, for the first time, Dominican-born managers faced each other in a game, and one was a former Red Sox catcher. Who was he?

115. Can you name the first Red Sox pitcher to allow six home runs in one game?

116. Who was the first Red Sox batting champ?

117. Major League players with what famous Red Sox player's last name have combined for the most home runs of any last name in baseball history?

118. Which one-time Red Sox pitcher was the first in baseball history to start World Series games in three different decades?

119. On April 9, 1912, the Red Sox made their first-ever appearance at Fenway Park—in an exhibition game against what opponent?

120. Who was the first president of the United States to attend a World Series game?

121. In what season did the Red Sox first use uniform numbers?

122. Who was the first Red Sox player to win the American League Rookie of the Year award?

123. Ron Bloomberg of the Yankees was the first designated hitter to bat in the American League. In his initial at bat he drew a walk from which Red Sox pitcher?

124. What one-time Red Sox pitcher was the first reliever to save 40 games in a single season in both the American and National leagues?

125. The first Latin-born Major League pitcher to throw a no-hitter was at one time a Red Sox player. Who was he?

126. Which one-time Red Sox pitcher was the first ever to have 100 saves and 100 complete games for his career?

127. Who was the first Red Sox starter since Rogelio Moret in 1975 to walk nine batters in a game?

128. Which Red Sox player was the first Major Leaguer signed by a team to be a designated hitter?

129. Who was the first one-time Red Sox player to win the National League Manager of the Year Award?

130. Who was the first one-time Red Sox player to win the American League Manager of the Year Award?

131. Which one-time Red Sox pitcher was the first to strike out at least 200 batters in eight consecutive seasons?

132. Which Red Sox player was the first to wear wrist sweatbands and lampblack under his eyes to reduce sun glare?

133. In April 1997, who did the Red Sox first introduce to loud boos from the Fenway crowd?

134. Which Red Sox player hit the first home run off the large Coke bottle above the Green Monster?

135. Which New York Yankee, playing his first game against the Red Sox, was the first player in the American League to get two hits in the same inning?

136. Who was the first Red Sox player to hit for the cycle twice in his career?

137. Which Sox Red player is one of three players to hit home runs in the All-Star game, the Divisional Championship, the League Championship, and the World Series, all in the same season?

138. Who was the first Red Sox pitcher to win the Cy Young Award?

139. In 2005 Albert Pujols became the first player since which Red Sox player to drive in at least 100 runs in each of his first five seasons?

140. Which Red Sox prospect, traded by the team, became the first player with six consecutive seasons with at least 30 home runs, 100 runs scored, 100 RBIs, and 100 walks?

141. Can you name the one-time Red Sox shortstop who was the first player elected to the Baseball Hall of Fame primarily for his defensive play?

142. The Red Sox' first team names were the Americans and the Somersets. By what nickname were the Sox known during the 1903 World Championship season?

143. Which National League team did Boston face in the first-ever World Series in 1903?

144. Which Red Sox pitcher is first—by far—in career complete games?

145. Which early Red Sox star was one of the first centerfielders to play a shallow centerfield with a runner on first base, allowing him to field a single and sometimes force the runner at second?

146. In what year did the Boston team first become known as the Red Sox?

147. Who hit the first home run in the history of Fenway Park?

148. Which Hall of Famer started and won the first game of the 1918 World Series for the Red Sox?

149. What Hall of Famer did owner Tom Yawkey hire as the first Red Sox general manager?

150. What was the real first name of Red Sox pitching great "Lefty" Grove?

151. Which former Red Sox draft pick was the first National Leaguer to steal 50 bases and score 110 runs in his rookie year?

152. Who was the first Red Sox player to have 130 career triples?

153. Which Hall of Fame pitcher, a former Red Sox standout, did Ted Williams face in his first Major League at bat?

154. Who was the first Red Sox player to win a Gold Glove Award?

155. Which Red Sox outfielder was the only man ever to pinch-hit for Ted Williams?

156. Who was the first Red Sox reliever to weigh at least 280 pounds?

157. In 1967 the Red Sox acquired the first African-American player in the history of the New York Yankees franchise. Who was he?

158. What is the full first name of former Red Sox star Rico Petrocelli?

159. Which former Red Sox manager had the nickname of a cartoon character?

160. Who was the first Red Sox slugger forced to retire from baseball because of vertigo?

161. Which Red Sox player, with a famous Boston political name, hit an inside-the-park home run in his first at bat with the Red Sox?

162. What Yankee reliever was first to ride in the Red Sox bullpen cart?

163. In what year did night baseball come to Boston?

164. Who were the first two Red Sox players to hit two grand-slam home runs in one game?

165. Which one-time Red Sox player was the first American League player to win the MVP award with two different teams?

166. Who was the first Red Sox manager to manage more than 2,000 games for the Red Sox?

167. Which Red Sox were the first pair of brothers to work together as pitcher and catcher in the Major Leagues?

168. When was the "Ted Williams shift"—with three infielders positioned on the right side of second base—first used?

169. Who was the first Red Sox right fielder to use sunglasses?

170. Who were the first three Red Sox pitchers to lead the American League in strikeouts for a season?

171. Can you name the first Red Sox player ever to have 12 consecutive hits?

172. Who were the first two pitchers in World Series history, both Red Sox players, to win three games in a single World Series?

173. Which former Red Sox player was the first Major League Baseball player to have been a collegiate football All-American?

174. Who is the first Red Sox player to have more than 300 career stolen bases?

175. Who were the first three African-American players to be given tryouts by the Red Sox in 1945?

176. What Red Sox pitcher was first to have 100-plus career saves?

177. Where was the first Red Sox training site in New England?

178. Name the first two father-and-son combinations to play for the Red Sox.

179. Which one-time Red Sox pitcher was the first and only man to pitch to both Babe Ruth and Mickey Mantle?

180. Who was the host of the first pregame radio quiz show from Fenway Park and Braves Field in the 1940s and 1950s?

181. Can you name the only two brothers to manage the Red Sox?

182. In 1957 who was the American League pitcher that Red Sox owner Tom Yawkey first offered a million dollars for?

183. Which pitcher threw the first Red Sox no-hitter in a night game?

184. Which two Red Sox catchers were first to catch two no-hitters each?

185. Name the player who was the first left-handed catcher for the Red Sox.

186. Can you name the first two Red Sox pitchers to win 20 games in a season during the 1960s?

187. What player did Ted Williams replace as the Red Sox regular left fielder?

188. Where did Carl Yastrzemski hit his first home run?

189. Before the team was officially called the Red Sox in 1907, what color were the club's first socks?

190. Where was the first Red Sox spring-training site?

191. Which two one-time Red Sox players were the first in baseball history to both pitch and play the outfield in different World Series?

192. Who was the Red Sox first free agent signing, following the first free agent draft in 1976?

193. Who was the first Red Sox shortstop to hit at least 40 home runs in a season?

194. Who was the Red Sox' first RBI champion, winning back-to-back titles in 1902 and 1903?

195. Which Red Sox player had 200-plus hits in each of his first three seasons, becoming the first Major League player to do so?

196. What was Carl Yastrzemski's position when signed by the Red Sox out of Notre Dame?

197. Who was the Red Sox pitcher to be credited with a perfect game he didn't start?

198. Who was the first player to have base hits in his first six at bats wearing a Sox uniform?

199. Which Red Sox player won the first three Gold Gloves for a third baseman?

200. Which Red Sox pitcher was the first reliever to strike out more than 180 batters in one season?

201. Name the former Red Sox player who was the first player to lead his league in errors at his position for seven years in a row.

202. Which Red Sox star was first to be honored with a player's day?

203. What Red Sox star became the first Sox player to retire because of a fear of flying?

204. What New Hampshire native and future star did the Red Sox select in the first round of the 1967 draft?

205. Which former Red Sox star was one of the first ten owners of the American Football League's Boston Patriots?

206. In 1999 what Red Sox relief pitcher's name was featured in the title of a best-selling novel?

207. The Red Sox were the only Major League team to have what recreational activity take place under their ballpark for 15 years?

208. In 2001 what pitcher, in his first start for the Red Sox, pitched a no-hitter against the Orioles in Camden Yards?

209. In 1980 what player became the first in Red Sox history to steal four bases in a game?

210. Which Red Sox manager was Michael Jordan's first minor league manager?

211. Who were the first two pitchers to get their 300th win as Red Sox?

212. When was a screen first installed atop the Green Monster to catch home run balls?

213. Who were the first two Red Sox players to play in 1,000 games at shortstop for the team?

214. Who was the first Red Sox reliever to reach 85 relief wins?

215. Which Red Sox player was the first unanimous American League Rookie of the Year?

216. Who was the first left-handed Red Sox pitcher to reach 120 career wins?

217. Which Red Sox was the first modern-day player to become a league president?

218. Who is the only Red Sox player—and one of only three players in Major League history—to steal bases in four decades?

219. Can you name the Red Sox player who was the first former Little League player to be elected to the MLB Hall of Fame?

220. Who were the first two Red Sox players to win the Silver Slugger Award, given annually to the best offensive player at each position in each league?

221. Who was the first Red Sox player to start a season with a 20-game hitting streak?

222. Which Red Sox infielder was the first Chicago Cub to homer at all four infield positions in one season?

223. Which Red Sox player is first all-time with a .370 lifetime average at Fenway Park (minimum 300 games)?

224. Which Red Sox reliever had nine blown saves in a season, after 1988 when such recordkeeping began?

225. Who was the first Sox player to have at least 900 career at bats for the Sox without ever hitting a triple?

226. Who was the Red Sox player described by rival manager Eddie Stanley of the White Sox as an "All-Star from the neck down"?

227. Which ex-Red Sox player was the first to hit 200 home runs in both the major and minor leagues?

228. Who was the first shortstop to replace Rick Burleson for the Red Sox in the early 1980s?

229. Which star pitcher left the Red Sox in the late 1980s because of the misbehavior of other Sox players while on road trips?

230. Who were the first three Red Sox players to have 10 RBIs in a single game?

231. Which Red Sox pitcher was first to have 20 or more wild pitches in a season?

232. Which Red Sox player was the first in team history to lead off nine games with home runs?

233. Can you name the first Red Sox player to change positions five times in one inning?

234. Can you name the first two Red Sox players with 10 or more letters in their last name to have hit 40 or more home runs in a season?

235. Which Red Sox left-handed hitter was the first to hit 28 home runs at Fenway Park in a season?

236. Which Red Sox player fought in World War II and the Korean War?

237. Can you name the first Red Sox player to have 240 hits in a season?

238. Which well-known one-time Red Sox pitcher was the first pitcher of the 1970s to win at least 14 games with five different teams?

239. Which Red Sox player had the team designate an area in centerfield where fans were required to wear dark clothes to improve the hitting background?

240. Who was the first Red Sox player banned from stock car racing by the team?

241. Can you name the first four left-handed Red Sox pitchers to win 70 percent of their decisions at Fenway Park?

242. Which Red Sox player is one of only four Major League players ever to hit three home runs in one game out of the ninth spot in the batting order?

243. Which player was the first Red Sox with more than 50 career pinch-hits?

244. What player was the first ever from Norwood, Massachusetts, to be a Red Sox free agent signing?

245. Who was the first Red Sox pitcher to win more than 30 games in a season?

246. Which former Red Sox player was the first pick of the Cleveland Browns football team in 1952?

247. Which Red Sox player hit the first grand-slam home run in an All-Star Game?

248. Who, in 1987, was the Red Sox pitcher arrested for stealing video cassettes from a store?

249. Who were the first three left-handed-hitting Red Sox rookies to hit 20 or more home runs in their rookie years?

250. Which three Red Sox outfielders were the first from one team to be the starting outfield in an All-Star game?

251. Which Red Sox pitcher was the first ever to lose a World Series game in which he hit a home run?

252. Who was the first Red Sox pitcher to have an errorless season with a minimum of 50 chances?

253. Which Red Sox player won eight Gold Gloves?

254. Which Red Sox was one of the first two players to have two pinch-hit home runs in a World Series?

255. Which Red Sox Hall of Famer was the first American League pitcher to record three consecutive 1-0 shutouts?

256. Which Red Sox pitcher was the first ever to begin a season 14-0?

257. Name the one-time Red Sox pitcher who is one of the first two Major League players to pitch a no-hitter in both leagues.

258. What Major League Baseball first was accomplished by the 1936 Boston Red Sox?

259. What pitcher was the first Korean to start a game for the Red Sox?

260. Who was the first Red Sox reliever to record saves in both games of a doubleheader sweep against the Yankees?

261. Who was the first Red Sox player fined by Major League Baseball for having too much pine tar on his batting helmet?

262. Who was the first Red Sox pitcher to record an All-Star Game victory?

263. What Red Sox star reached 100 career home runs at the earliest age?

264. Who were the first two Red Sox players to have two home runs in their first two games?

265. In 1992 what Sox player stole home in a game against Toronto, becoming the first Red Sox since Joe Foy, in 1968, to do so?

266. In 1980 what Sox pitcher played left field for one out in the ninth inning, becoming the first Red Sox pitcher to play another position in the field since Mike Ryba caught three games in 1942?

267. Can you name the only two Red Sox players to hit multiple home runs on their birthdays (both times in the early 2000s)?

268. In 1992 what actor bid $93,500 at auction for the ball hit by Mookie Wilson that went through Bill Buckner's legs in game 6 of the 1986 World Series?

269. Can you name the first three Red Sox players to hit 30-plus home runs in three consecutive years?

270. Who was the Red Sox player hit by a pitch 35 times in a season?

271. Who was the first Red Sox reliever to have 12 saves in a month?

272. Can you name the Red Sox player who was first to have 53 hits in one month?

273. Who was the first Red Sox player to play for the Harlem Globetrotters?

274. Which Red Sox pitcher had 113 starts with the team but never registered a shutout?

275. Who was the first Red Sox pitcher to allow 38 home runs in a season?

276. Which one-time Red Sox player was first to hit for the cycle in each league?

277. Who was the first Red Sox player to strike out more than 160 times in one season?

278. Can you name the 290–pound Red Sox first baseman from the Virgin Islands? (He played during the 2001 season.)

279. Who was the first Red Sox player to ride a police horse on the field at Fenway?

280. Who was the first Red Sox pitcher to strike out 12 batters in a relief appearance?

281. Which Red Sox player had the lowest season batting average of anyone in baseball history to drive in more than 100 runs in the same season?

282. Who was the first Red Sox player to have a bill bearing his name proposed by the Massachusetts House of Representatives?

283. When Mel Parnell won his 25th game in 1949, he became the first Red Sox left-hander to win 25 games. Whose record of 24 wins did he surpass?

284. What Red Sox manager, according to an article in *Penthouse*, was first to be the subject of FBI scrutiny for betting on football and basketball?

285. Who is the only Red Sox right-handed hitter ever to bat over .370?

286. Name the first Red Sox shortstop to drive in 100 runs since Rico Petrocelli did it in 1970.

287. Which Red Sox player was the first American Leaguer to have 23 game-winning hits in a season?

288. Which Red Sox player had a brand of bread named after him?

289. Which Red Sox pitcher was the first 19-year-old to pitch in a World Series?

290. Who was the first Red Sox player named American League MVP, even though he was in the U.S. Army before the season was over?

291. Can you name the Red Sox player who was the first three-time winner of the American League MVP award?

292. Which Red Sox player was fined $15 for a duck-hunting violation?

293. In 1934 Joe Cronin's first official act as Red Sox manager was to appoint whom to coach third base?

294. Name the Red Sox player who had a tunnel named after him.

295. What Red Sox player was the first Cy Young Award winner to be injured in a skiing accident?

296. Who was the first and only Red Sox manager to be sent to prison?

297. In 1965 which Red Sox star introduced a single titled "Why Don't They Understand"?

298. Which Major League team first drafted future Red Sox star Fred Lynn?

299. What Red Sox public-address announcer wrote a classic 1960s rock-and-roll hit?

300. Who was the first Red Sox pitcher to have five perfect games?

301. What Red Sox pitcher, in 1970, struck out the first six men he faced in a game to tie a Major League record?

302. Name the Red Sox player who was the first switch-hitter to strike out more than 175 times in a season.

303. The first seat painted red at Fenway Park is in the right-field bleachers. What does it signify?

304. Which one-time Red Sox pitcher was first to throw both left-handed and right-handed to one batter?

305. Which player, with the Red Sox at the end of his career, was first to regularly wear a helmet in the field?

306. Which one-time Red Sox was the first player to have his number retired by the Tampa Bay Devil Rays?

307. Which Red Sox player in uniform was the first Korean American in Major League Baseball?

308. Which one-time Red Sox player was the first in baseball history to run the bases backward?

309. Name the Red Sox pitcher who was first to go 20-1 during a season. He was with another team at the time.

310. Which Red Sox player, traded to the Yankees, was the first to call Yankee Stadium "the Bronx Zoo"?

311. Which one-time Red Sox manager was first to win a pennant with three different teams and finish first in all of baseball's divisions? (There were four divisions at the time.)

312. Which one-time Red Sox manager was the first rookie manager to win a World Series?

313. Which pitcher, acquired by the Red Sox at the end of his career, was the first Canadian-born player inducted into the Baseball Hall of Fame?

314. Which one-time Red Sox first baseman was the first player to return to Major League baseball after playing in Japan?

315. Which one-time Red Sox manager was the New York Mets' first third baseman?

316. Which Red Sox outfielder was the first player in history responsible for all his team's runs in a game in which the team scored nine runs?

317. Which Red Sox pitcher was the first in Major League history to win three clinching games in a single postseason?

318. Which Red Sox player acquired late in his career was the first Major League player to receive five intentional walks in a single game?

319. Which Red Sox star was the first American League player to walk six times in a nine-inning game?

320. Which Red Sox player was the first to hit 50 or more home runs in a season yet fail to lead his league in home runs?

321. Which Red Sox player was first to lead his league in hits in the first three seasons in which he appeared in the Majors?

322. Which Red Sox player is the only Major League player with more than 3,000 career hits but no 200-hit seasons?

323. Which one-time Red Sox player was the first Canadian to hit 20 or more home runs in four consecutive years?

324. Name the first five Red Sox players with 20 home runs and 20 steals in a season.

325. Which Red Sox player was the first visiting player ever to have consecutive two–home run games against the Yankees at Yankee Stadium?

326. Which Red Sox player was first to lead his league in steals in one year while stealing only 100 bases in his entire career?

327. What Red Sox player was the first since the early 1900s to post a sub-.900 fielding average?

328. Who were the first three Red Sox players to steal 30 or more bases in successive seasons?

329. Who was the first two-time batting champ since 1965 to manage the Red Sox for a short time?

330. Can you name the first three African-Americans to play for the Red Sox?

331. Which Red Sox pitcher was one of the first two pitchers to make 25 starts in a year after amassing at least 80 career saves?

332. Can you name the first four Red Sox pitchers to hit grand-slam home runs?

333. What Red Sox player was the first ever to hit grand slams from both sides of the plate in the same game?

334. Who was the first Red Sox player to finish in the top four of the Heisman Trophy voting?

335. Who were the first two Red Sox players to have 40 RBIs in one month?

336. The first game at Fenway Park in 1912 was overshadowed by what major world event?

337. Which player, later with the Red Sox, was the first rookie pitcher ever to make an All-Star team while pitching for an expansion team?

338. Which Red Sox player was the first player ever to hit the first pitch of a season for a home run?

339. Which Red Sox player was first to lead his league in home runs, triples, and RBIs in the same season?

340. Who were the first two Red Sox players to be on a *Sports Illustrated* cover?

341. Which Red Sox infield was the first of only two infields in baseball history to finish a season with at least 20 home runs each for the first baseman, second baseman, third baseman, and shortstop?

342. Who were the first two Red Sox pitchers to win the pitching Triple Crown (wins, strikeouts, and ERA)?

343. Which Red Sox pitcher was the first Cy Young Award winner to give up eight runs in a league championship game?

344. Which Red Sox player is one of the first two Boston-area athletes to be pictured shirtless on a *Sports Illustrated* cover?

345. Can you name the one-time Red Sox player who was the first Major Leaguer to be caught stealing twice in the same inning?

346. Which Red Sox pitching coach had been the first National League player to hit two grand-slam home runs in one game?

347. In the ten-year period 1954–1963, the Yankees had the MVP winner eight times. Which Red Sox player was one of the two non-Yankees to win the MVP in that decade?

348. Which Red Sox was the first American League first baseman to win the Rookie of the Year Award?

349. Which one-time Red Sox player is credited with inventing the "bat doughnut" for warming up in the on-deck circle?

350. Which pitcher, later with the Red Sox, was one of three pitchers to win a deciding game against the Yankees in the World Series by throwing a shutout at Yankee Stadium?

351. Who were the first three Red Sox players to hit walk-off home runs in the postseason?

352. Which one-time Red Sox was the first pitcher with a minimum of 175 innings to have more wins than walks issued in one season?

353. Which one-time Red Sox player was first to be a member of four All-Star teams before he earned a regular Major League job?

354. Which Red Sox player was first to order a bat with a knob on the end of the handle?

355. Which Red Sox pitcher was first to give up only four total hits in two consecutive World Series complete-game wins?

356. Which Red Sox pitcher was the first to win a Gold Glove?

357. Which Red Sox player was first to strike out six times in a 15-inning game?

358. Which one-time Red Sox player was one of only two players in baseball history with over 3,000 career hits—who also pitched in a game while over the age of 40?

359. Name the one-time Red Sox who was the first player since 1900 to have 14 hits over three consecutive games.

360. Which one-time Red Sox player was the first Hall of Famer to play more than 2,500 games at just one position for his entire career?

361. Which Red Sox manager is one of the first four men in uniform to have been ejected from games in six different decades?

362. Which Red Sox player was the first Venezuelan elected to the Baseball Hall of Fame?

363. What one-time Red Sox player was first to appear in one World Series as a pitcher and another World Series as an outfielder?

364. Which Red Sox team member, in uniform in 2006, was half of the father-and-son duo that played for the most different teams in their careers?

365. Who was the Red Sox player to have his model bat used in a famous movie that starred Jack Nicholson?

366. Which short-term Sox player was the first to tie three of baseball's most famous records in one day?

367. Which Red Sox player is one of the first two repeat winners of the *Sports Illustrated* Sportsman of the Year Award?

368. Which Red Sox star was first to have a main character in a famous sports movie based on him?

369. Two Major League players, one a Red Sox, won the first 19 Gold Gloves at one position. Who were the two players and what was their position?

370. Which Red Sox player wore a Beatles wig to the plate at Kansas City?

371. Which Red Sox great still leads the Major Leagues in career assists for an outfielder?

372. Which one-time Red Sox pitcher was the first reliever to appear in half his team's games in one season?

373. Name the famous Red Sox player who was one of only three men to play in the 1960s, 1970s, 1980s, and 1990s.

374. Of five Major League pitchers with a 20-win season and a 20-save season, three were at one time Red Sox. Can you name them?

375. Which one-time Red Sox pitcher was first to play for three pro sports teams in the same city?

376. Name the Red Sox player who is among the first three switch-hitters ever with at least 100 home runs in each league.

377. Which Red Sox reliever was the first pitcher to save 30 games in a season for three different teams?

378. Which one-time Red Sox pitcher was among the first three Hall of Fame pitchers to bat in the American League after the introduction in 1973 of the designated hitter?

379. Which Red Sox outfielder is one of the first two men to have played in the All-Star game and the World Series in both leagues?

380. Which Red Sox Hall of Famer was the first American Leaguer to strike out five times in one game?

381. Which one-time Red Sox player was the first unanimous selection as the National League's MVP?

382. Which one-time Red Sox pitcher popularized the high leg kick?

383. Which Red Sox great played right field with eyeliner and mascara?

PATR

NEW ENGLAND PATRIOTS

1. Two of the first three NFL running backs to average 100 yards rushing per game for a season were Jim Brown and Jim Taylor. A Patriot was the third. Who was he?

2. Which Patriot, active in 2006, is the cousin of a Major League Baseball player and an NBA forward?

3. Which Pats player, with at least 50 games with the team, is ranked in the top 10 on the team's all-time receiving, kick-off return, and punt return lists?

4. Which Patriots player was among the first three NFL players with at least one interception and 15 pass receptions in an NFL season?

5. Who was the first Patriot to recover five opponent fumbles in one season?

6. Can you name the first three Patriots to record four sacks in one game?

7. Who was the first Patriot to average more than 30 yards per kick-off return in a season?

8. Who are the first three Patriot running backs to have more than 1,000 rushes in their career?

9. Who was the first Patriot to return two interceptions for touchdowns in one game?

10. Who was the first Patriot to recover 17 opponent fumbles in his career?

11. Which Patriot had 10 sacks in his rookie year?

12. Who was the first Patriot to score 18 points in a playoff game?

13. Which local quarterback was the number-one pick of the Patriots in the 1964 AFL draft?

14. Who was the first Patriot selected as the Associated Press Defensive Rookie of the Year?

15. Which Patriots player needed 2.5 sacks in 2006 to become the first player in NFL history to post 30 interceptions and 30 sacks?

16. Which Patriot is the first NFL player to record two touchdowns and a sack in the same game?

17. Which 2006 player was the first Patriot to appear on a reality TV show?

18. Which former Patriots kicker was the first college kicker to connect on two 60-yard field goals in one game?

19. Who was the first Patriot to have 145 consecutive starts for the team?

20. Who was the first Patriot to run for at least one touchdown in seven consecutive games?

21. Which player began the 1998 season by rushing for at least one touchdown in each of the Patriots' first six games?

22. Who was the first Patriot to catch at least one pass in more than 60 consecutive games?

23. Who were the first two running backs named to the Patriots' "Team of the Century" in 2003?

24. Who were the first Patriots to catch two touchdown passes in a postseason game?

25. Which Patriots quarterback was first to play in an AFL All-Star Game?

26. Which Patriots running back was first to play in an AFL All-Star Game?

27. Who was the first Patriots kicker to average more than 45 yards per punt in a season?

28. Who are the first two Patriots to return multiple kickoffs for touchdowns in one season?

29. Which Patriot, playing for another team, was the first player to score touchdowns on a fumble return, an interception return, and a kickoff return in the same season?

30. Which Patriot caught the first touchdown pass in Gillette Stadium history?

31. Who are the first three Patriots to have more than 72 career sacks?

32. Name the first three Patriots placekickers to be named to the Pro Bowl.

33. Which Patriot was the first defensive player to score a touchdown in the Super Bowl since William "The Refrigerator" Perry in 1986?

34. Which female reporter was the first to be involved in a locker-room incident with a Patriots player?

35. Can you name the first four Heisman Trophy winners to play for the Patriots?

36. Which two Patriots were first to have five consecutive games with a receiving touchdown?

37. Who was the first player in Patriots history to return a missed field goal for a touchdown?

38. Who were the first two Patriots quarterbacks to throw five touchdown passes in one game?

39. Which one-time Patriot was the first NFL receiver to play with 18 quarterbacks in his career and catch touchdown passes from each of them?

40. Can you name the first person on work release from prison to aid the Patriots in a victory?

41. Who was the first Patriot to have 50 career fumbles?

42. Which Patriot worked at Disneyland as a dwarf?

43. Can you name the first Patriots quarterback with 30 or more touchdown passes in one season?

44. Who was the first Patriots owner involved in personal-care products?

45. Which Patriot was first with 16 receptions in a single game?

46. Which Patriot was the first player ever to return four consecutive interceptions for touchdowns?

47. Which two Patriots had more than 70 catches each in the same year?

48. Where was the Patriots' first home game played?

49. Which one-time Patriot was the first player to win a Heisman Trophy, be a number-one overall draft pick, and be a Super Bowl MVP winner?

50. Who were the first three Patriots wide receivers since 1970 to be selected to the Pro Bowl?

51. Which three Patriots were first to run back two punts for touchdowns in one season?

52. Which Patriot made the first interception in Gillette Stadium history?

53. Which Patriot player is one of two players, along with O.J. Simpson, to rush for more than 245 yards in a game twice in his career?

54. Who was the first Patriot to record three 80-catch seasons?

55. Which Patriot was first to average over 14.5 yards per punt return in one season?

56. Which Patriot, active in 2006, was first in NCAA career sacks as of 2006?

57. Which player was the first Patriots kicker to average almost 45 yards per punt in his career?

58. Can you name the Patriot who was first to rush for more than 210 yards in a single game?

59. Which Patriot was first in team history to score 28 points in a single game?

60. Which 2006 Patriot was the first Patriot to win, in 1999, the Dan Hodge Award, known as the Heisman Trophy of wrestling?

61. Name the Patriots player who held 16 Cincinnati Bengals records at one time.

62. Which Patriots player was drafted in 1996 by baseball's Florida Marlins?

63. Richard Seymour is the first Patriot to earn at least three Pro Bowl nods in his first four seasons since which two other Patriots?

64. Can you name the Patriot not named Cappelletti or Nance who was the team's first season scoring leader?

65. Can you name the first four Patriots to record more than 1,000 yards on kick-off returns in a season?

66. Which Patriot was first to be an MVP in the Pro Bowl?

67. Doug Flutie's drop-kick extra point for the Patriots in 2006 was the first drop-kick in the NFL in how many years?

68. Which Patriots player was the first to make a snow angel after the Patriots victory over Oakland in the 2001 divisional playoffs?

69. Which Patriot, when in high school, wrestled future Heisman winner Ricky Williams?

70. Which Patriot attended the same high school as a pro football Hall of Famer and a likely future baseball Hall of Famer?

71. Which Patriot, while playing for another team, broke a 40-year-old NFL rookie rushing record set by Hall of Famer Jim Brown?

72. Who was the first Patriot to have 40 carries in a game?

73. Which future NFL coach played linebacker for the Patriots in 1969–70?

74. Name the rookie who started for the Patriots on kickoff weekend in 2005.

75. Which Patriot had his career derailed by a knee injury suffered during a beach competition at the Pro Bowl in 1998?

76. Who was the first Patriot to have a one-game rushing average of more than 11.5 yards per carry (minimum of 10 carries)?

77. Who was the first Patriot to catch 10 touchdown passes in a single season?

78. Who was the Patriots' starting quarterback in the first season that they were known as the "New England Patriots"?

79. Who was the first Patriots running back to make the Pro Bowl?

80. Which Patriot was first to make the Pro Bowl as a special-teams player?

81. Which Patriot was the first elected to the Pro Bowl as a kick returner?

82. Which Patriot was first to catch a touchdown pass in five consecutive games?

83. Who was the first starting quarterback in Patriots history to go six consecutive games without an interception?

84. Can you name the first three Patriots running backs with 11 receptions in a single game?

85. Which player was the first in Patriots history to record two safeties in one season?

86. Which team did the Patriots beat on kickoff weekend in 1971 in their very first home game at Schaefer Stadium?

87. Name the Patriot who was first to average more than 27 yards on kickoff returns in one season (minimum of 20 returns).

88. Which Patriots linebacker is first in the number of times he was selected for the Pro Bowl?

89. Name the two players with 200 or more games for the Patriots.

90. Which Patriot was listed as questionable on a pre–Super Bowl injury report because a tendon in his finger was sliced in a knife accident?

91. What was the first pro team for future Patriot Doug Flutie in 1985 after leaving Boston College?

92. When was a natural-grass playing surface installed at Foxboro Stadium?

93. Which Patriot was first to attempt 70 passes in a single game?

94. Which Patriot was first to have an 85-yard run from scrimmage?

95. What was the first position played as a pro by Patriots all-time great kicker-receiver Gino Cappelletti?

96. Who was the first Patriot credited with more than 205 tackles in a season?

97. Who was the first Patriot to rush for 100 yards in a game?

98. Can you name the first Patriot to have 200 yards receiving in a game?

99. Which Patriot was first to amass 100 yards receiving in a game?

100. Who was the first Patriot to return a punt for a touchdown?

101. Which Patriot is first in years of service to the team, with 16 seasons as a player?

102. Which Patriots coach is one of two coaches to have back-to-back 14-win regular seasons?

103. Over the 2003 and 2004 seasons, the Patriots scored first in how many consecutive regular-season games?

104. Which Patriot was first to catch 50 passes in a season?

105. Who was the first Patriots linebacker to play in five consecutive AFL All-Star games?

106. Which Patriot was called greatest-ever at his position by *Sports Illustrated*?

107. Who was the first Patriots Hall of Famer to have played college football at Alabama?

108. Which Patriot was first to pass for three touchdowns in a postseason game?

109. Who was the first Patriots kicker with a punt over 65 yards in a postseason game?

110. Which Patriots All-Star linebacker attended North Dakota State University?

111. Can you name the Patriot who had the first kickoff return over 45 yards in Patriots postseason history?

112. Which 2004 Patriots opponent was the first team in more than three years to defeat the Patriots after trailing at the half?

113. Which Patriot recorded the 100th sack of his career in his final game as a Patriot?

114. Who was the first Patriot to lead the team or be tied for the team lead in interceptions for a record six consecutive seasons, from 1989 through 1994?

115. Who were the first two Patriots running backs to lead the team in yards from scrimmage four times?

116. Who was the first running back to lead the Patriots in receptions in one season?

117. Which Patriot was first to return an interception for a touchdown in a postseason game?

118. Can you name the famous person who gave Patriots tight end Russ Francis the nickname "All World"?

119. Who was Tom Brady's first backup at quarterback in 2004?

120. Which Patriots team was first to average more than 370 yards per game in total offense?

121. Who was the first in Patriots history to return a fumble recovery over 65 yards for a touchdown?

122. Before Drew Bledsoe took over as Patriots quarterback in 1993, who started four games at quarterback?

123. Who was the first coach to lead SMU to a Southwest Conference championship, before becoming Patriots coach in 1982?

124. Which future star did the Patriots take with first overall pick in the 1984 draft?

125. Who was the first Patriot to return an interception for a touchdown in the 2004 regular season?

126. Name the first Patriot to average over 20 yards per catch in his career.

127. Which player, drafted out of Kansas State in the fifth round in 1975, went on to a 16-year career with the Patriots?

128. Can you name the Patriot who was first to accumulate 10,000 career receiving yards?

129. Who was the first Patriot to earn nine Pro Bowl selections?

130. Who was the first Patriots player to officially sign a contract with the team?

131. Before the team moved to Gillette Stadium in 2002, how many years had the Patriots played at Foxboro Stadium?

132. Which NFL team beat the Patriots in 2004 to end a record 18-game winning streak?

133. Name the Patriot who was first to rush for more than 1,400 yards in one AFL season.

134. Who were the first four principal owners in Patriots history?

135. Which Patriot was named for a former NFL quarterback?

136. Which Patriot rushed for 144 yards in the first postseason game of his career?

137. Which coach was first to take the Patriots to the Super Bowl?

138. Which team was the Patriots' first regular-season opponent?

139. Name the player the Patriots selected in the first round of the 1991 draft. He ranked fourth in the AFC in rushing yards in his rookie season.

140. Can you name the former Patriot whose father was a four-time Pro Bowl defensive tackle?

141. Which Patriot was the first ever to rush for 100 yards or more in consecutive playoff games?

142. Who were the first two Patriots to combine on a pass completion over 90 yards?

143. Which Patriot was first to have a run from scrimmage of greater than 75 yards during a playoff game?

144. Which unlikely Patriot was first to lead the team in interceptions?

145. Who was the first Patriot to average 15.5 yards per punt return in a season?

146. Name the Patriot who was drafted by baseball's Montreal Expos in 1995.

147. Which Patriot was on a Little League team that lost in the Little League World Series final to Venezuela?

148. Which Patriot was a member of the first tandem in Division I-A history to gain more than 1,000 yards rushing each in consecutive seasons?

149. Can you name the first Patriot to record an interception and a reception in the same game?

150. Which Patriot is one of the first three players all-time in Super Bowl receptions, entering 2006?

151. Which Patriot was the first rookie guard since John Hannah in 1974 to start every game in his rookie season?

152. When did the Patriots' first victory take place?

153. Which Patriot was the first player in AFL history to score more than 1,000 points in his career?

154. Who was the first radio voice of the Patriots?

155. Who was the first Harvard product to play for the Patriots?

156. Who were the first brothers to play for the Patriots?

157. Which Patriots quarterback in 1971 refused to sign his player's contract because of the reserve clause and walked out of training camp to return to his home near Boston?

158. Who was the Patriots Hall of Famer whose brother and father both played professional football?

159. Which Patriots player scored the first points ever in the AFL and then never scored again?

160. Where was the first Patriots training camp held?

161. Who scored the Patriots' first regular-season touchdown?

162. Name the first NFL stadium named after a brand of beer.

163. Who was the first Patriot to score touchdowns rushing, receiving, and returning a kickoff in one season?

164. Who were the first two Patriots players to score more than 100 points in the same season?

165. Who was the first Patriots player to return a kickoff 100 or more yards for a touchdown?

166. Who was the first Patriot to record four sacks in a game?

167. Which ex-Patriot was the first quarterback in Super Bowl history to have none of his passing attempts intercepted (minimum of 40 attempts)?

168. Who was the first Patriots rookie back to score multiple rushing touchdowns in a single game?

169. Name the Heisman Trophy winner from Navy who played for the Patriots.

170. Which one-time Patriot was the first player to quarterback a team in a Rose Bowl, a Grey Cup, and a Super Bowl?

171. Who was the first Patriots player to have his name on a brand of food?

172. Which Patriots coach was among the first five coaches to take two different teams to the Super Bowl?

173. Which Patriot is one of two players in NFL history to reach the 100-point mark in each of his first eight years in the league?

174. Which Patriot was the first Heisman Trophy winner to throw more than 300 touchdown passes in his pro career?

175. Which Patriot is among the first four quarterbacks to throw four interceptions in a Super Bowl game?

176. Which one-time Patriots player made appearances on TV's *The Rookies* and *Adam 12*?

177. The most popular retired jersey number in the NFL is 14. Who was the Patriot who had the number 14 retired?

178. Which was the first season in Patriots history when the team was undefeated at home?

179. In what year did Patriots season-ticket sales eclipse 40,000 for the first time?

180. When did the Patriots repeat as division champions for the first time in franchise history?

181. Which Patriots coach was first to be with the team for more than 22 seasons?

182. Which Patriots head coach coached less than one season?

183. Which former member of the Patriots coaching staff was first ever to be elected to the NFL's All-Decade team for the 1940s and be listed as one of the NFL's 300 greatest players?

184. Name the Patriots full-color weekly publication, the first offered by an NFL team.

185. Which ex-Patriot star was first cousin to daredevil Evel Knievel?

186. With what NFL team did Bill Belichick begin his coaching career?

187. Which Patriot hosted *Saturday Night Live*?

188. In a game against Denver in 2001, Tom Brady threw his first career interception after how many attempts without an interception?

189. In a game against Miami in December 2001, Tom Brady caught his first career pass from which Patriots teammate?

190. In 2000 Tom Brady completed his first NFL pass to which player?

191. Name the Patriot veteran who made his first trip to the Pro Bowl in 2001.

192. Which Patriot had the first special-teams return for a score in the playoffs in franchise history and the first punt return for a score in AFC championship history?

193. Troy Brown's first career interception came at the expense of which familiar quarterback?

194. Name the captain of the 2003 Patriots defense which became the first defensive unit in 65 years not to allow a touchdown in four consecutive home games in one season.

195. Which Patriot was the first linebacker in Chicago Bears history to record back-to-back double-digit sack seasons?

196. Which Patriot was the first player in LSU history to rush for more than 1,000 yards in a season three times in his college career?

197. Which Patriot player served as honorary ringmaster for the Big Apple Circus in 2004?

198. Which ex-Patriot owned his own entertainment company in Los Angeles, called "55 Entertainment"?

199. Which Patriot player began his pro football career in the Canadian Football League (CFL) in 1994-95 with the Baltimore Stallions?

200. Which Patriot was one of the first two NFL players born in South Dakota?

201. Which Patriot is a native of Brantford, Ontario, the home of hockey great Wayne Gretzky?

202. Which Patriot was featured in an HBO documentary filmed in 1999–2000?

203. Who was the first executive hired by the Patriots? He was also the Patriots' second head coach.

BOSTON CELTICS

1. Which one-time Celtic is credited with being first to break a backboard in the NBA?

2. Which Celtic hit the double-overtime shot in the 1957 championship series against the St. Louis Hawks to give the Celtics their first NBA championship?

3. Which Celtic was the first pro athlete to win a championship ring in two major sports?

4. Which Celtic asked that his retirement celebration be held with no fans, only ex-teammates, in attendance?

5. Which Celtic was the first guard to win the NBA's MVP award?

6. Who was the Celtics' first NBA Finals MVP?

7. Who was the first African-American player drafted by the Celtics?

8. Who was the first Celtic to host *Saturday Night Live*?

9. What item did Celtics announcer Johnny Most have retired by a Boston team?

10. Who was first to be head coach of both the Boston Celtics and Boston University?

11. Who was the first man to play for the Celtics, the Dodgers, and the Cubs—but was better known as a TV star?

12. Who was the first Toronto Blue Jay to play for the Celtics?

13. Which future Celtic was the first NCAA Division I college basketball player to score 3,000 points in his career?

14. Who was the first Celtic to win an NBA scoring title (highest average points per game)?

15. Whose number was first to be retired by the Celtics?

16. Which Celtic won the first NBA three-point shooting contest?

17. Which Celtic player replaced Bill Russell at center in 1969?

18. What future NBA head coach was the Celtics' first pick in the 1972 NBA draft?

19. When was the first regular-season Celtics game played at the Fleet Center?

20. Which Celtic had the first four-point play in team history?

21. Who was the Celtics' first seven-foot player?

22. Who was the Celtics' first coach?

23. Who were the first two Celtics to record 500 rebounds and 500 assists in a single season?

24. What feat did the Celtics accomplish on February 25, 1949?

25. Which Celtic was first to lead the NBA in total points?

26. The Celtics were the first team to give up 100 points per game for a season. In which season did they do so?

27. The 1961–62 Celtics became the first NBA team to set a milestone of how many wins?

28. In 1959 the Celtics became the first team to sweep an opponent in the NBA Finals. What team did they defeat?

29. Which Celtic was the first NBA player to score 1,000 or more points for 16 consecutive seasons?

30. Who was the first Celtic to win the NBA MVP award three or more consecutive times?

31. Which Celtic was the first NBA player to win eight consecutive assist titles?

32. Which Celtic was the first NBA player unofficially referred to as a "sixth man"?

33. Which Celtic great did the team select in the first round of the 1956 draft, after the Rochester Royals passed on him?

34. Which Celtics star coached the Lakers to their first NBA championship after they had moved from Minneapolis to Los Angeles?

35. Which Celtic center had 40 rebounds in each of three NBA playoff games?

36. Name a player who was a teammate of both Bill Russell and Larry Bird.

37. Who was the first Celtic to go from an NCAA championship team to an NBA championship team?

38. The first two coaches to both play on an NCAA championship team and coach an NBA championship team were Celtics. Can you name them?

39. In 1963 Celtics numbers 14 and 22 were the first retired. Which players wore those numbers?

40. Which one-time Celtic was the first NCAA player to average over 44 points per game in one collegiate season?

41. Which Celtics player was the first coach to win championships in the ABL, the ABA, and the NBA?

42. Which former Celtics All-Star was first to win a season-long game of H-O-R-S-E among NBA stars in the 1970s?

43. Which former Celtic and his son were the first basketball father and son to be on separate *Sports Illustrated* covers?

44. What former Celtic is the first player in NBA history with 20,000 points, 8,000 assists, and 2,000 steals in his career?

45. During the playing of the national anthem at Boston Garden, which Celtic looked for inspiration at Bobby Orr's retired jersey hanging in the rafters?

46. Which Celtic is credited with being the first player to use bump-and-run pass coverage in a professional football training camp tryout?

47. Which Celtic was the first pro basketball player to appear on a Wheaties box?

48. Name the first brewery to own the Celtics.

49. Can you name the first brothers to play together for the Celtics?

50. Which Celtics star was the first person who never played in a Major League Baseball game but was thrown out of one?

51. Celtic KC Jones's first NBA coaching job was as an assistant with which team?

52. What former NBA scoring champ was acquired by the Celtics after a suggestion by the owner's wife?

53. Who was the first Celtics draftee to agree to terms by transatlantic telephone?

54. What former New England college star was moved by the Celtics to make room for Bill Russell's return from the 1956 Olympics?

55. Who were the first four Celtics to make the NBA's All-Rookie team since its inception in 1963–64?

56. Who was the Celtics' first center?

57. Which Celtics number-one draft pick was cut because of his refusal to fly in an airplane?

58. KC Jones first became a Celtics assistant coach under which head coach?

59. What team did the Celtics defeat in the 1981 NBA Finals for Bill Fitch's NBA title?

60. Can you name the Celtic who was first to play for NCAA and ABA championship teams?

61. Who was the first Celtic to have his nickname, instead of his number, retired to the Boston Garden rafters?

62. Which Celtic, when the team won the 1974 NBA championship, was found sleeping on a Boston Common bench the following night?

63. Who was the first Boston College graduate to play for the Celtics?

64. What feat were the Celtics the first to accomplish when they won the 1964 championship?

65. NBA rebounding statistics were kept starting in the 1950–51 season. Which Celtic was first in rebounds four of the first five years these statistics were kept?

66. The Celtics' first regular-season game on November 2, 1946, was played in which New England city?

67. Who was the first Northeastern product to play for the Celtics?

68. What team did the Celtics defeat for their first-ever win?

69. Which Celtic was the team's first NBA Rookie of the Year?

70. The Celtics were the first NBA team to put an all African-American team on the court. Can you name the players?

71. Who was the first Celtic to be traded?

72. Who was first to collect playoff shares from the Celtics as well as the Red Sox and the Bruins?

73. Who was first to play for the Celtics, the Boston Braves, and the Red Sox?

74. Which former Celtic was the first guard in NBA history to score 1,000 field goals in a season?

75. In 1986 Larry Bird became the first NBA player ever voted what award?

76. What was the first name of Celtics legend "Red" Auerbach?

77. Name the first three Celtics to lead the NBA in free-throw percentage.

78. Which Celtic was the first NBA player to play past the age of 40?

79. Who was the first Celtic to play college basketball for Centenary, where he was a star player?

80. What team did Celtic John Havlicek play on with all-time greats Oscar Robertson and Jerry West?

81. Who played basketball with the Celtics, hockey with the Bruins, football with the Detroit Lions, and soccer with the Tampa Bay Rowdies?

82. Who was the first player-coach to win a title with the Celtics?

83. Which Celtic was the first NBA player to get 28 assists in one game?

84. Who was the first Celtic to score 60 points in a game?

85. Which one-time Celtic wore the same pair of socks in every game of college basketball he played for four years?

86. Which Celtic became the first African-American head coach in pro sports?

87. Which Celtics coach was the first coach to be ejected from an All-Star game?

88. Which Celtic was first to average 25 points per game for a season?

89. Who was the first Celtic elected to the Basketball Hall of Fame?

90. Which Celtic registered the first three-point basket in an All-Star game?

91. Which Celtic was the first seven-footer to use the jump shot as his main offensive weapon?

92. Who was the first Celtic to play more than 1,200 games in his career?

93. Name the first Celtic to score more than 40 points in a game.

94. Which Celtic was the first "60-80" player in an NBA season? (He made more than 60% of field goals and more than 80% of free throws attempted.)

95. What is the first name of Celtics coach "Doc" Rivers?

96. What Celtic was the first NBA player to introduce the shoot-around as a way to prepare for games?

97. In 1970 what team eliminated the Celtics from the playoffs for the first time in 20 years?

98. Can you name the Celtic who declined his election to the Basketball Hall of Fame? (He later reconsidered and accepted the honor.)

99. Which Celtic has two streets named in his honor?

100. Which Celtics coach was first to have a trophy named after him?

101. Who were the first two Celtics to win the NBA's Sixth Man Award?

102. Which Celtic was the first NBA MVP award winner who had not been selected to the All-NBA First Team in the same year?

103. Who was the first one-time Celtic to win the NBA scoring championship with another team?

104. Which Celtic had the NBA's highest field goal percentage in two seasons?

105. Who was the first one-time Celtic to have the highest three-point field goal percentage in a season?

106. As of the start of the 2006 season, which Celtic is first in career games played?

107. Which Celtics player was the leading scorer in the first NBA All-Star game, played on March 2, 1951, at the Boston Garden?

108. Which Celtics coach was the first college basketball coach to reach the NCAA Final Four with three different college teams?

109. Who was the first Celtic to have more than 60 triple doubles (10+ points, rebounds, and assists in a game)?

110. Which one-time Celtic was the first New Orleans Jazz player to lead the NBA in scoring?

111. Can you name the first five Celtics coaches to win NBA championships?

112. Which Celtic was first to win both Rookie of the Year and Coach of the Year awards in the NBA?

113. Of the first four NBA forwards to win NBA MVP awards, two were Celtics. Can you name them? (One played only part of his career in Boston.)

114. Which Celtic was the only NBA player in the 1980s to play in both the NBA and Major League Baseball?

115. Bob Cousy of the Celtics was a first-team All-Star for how many consecutive seasons?

116. What former Celtic was among the first five NBA players to lead the league at least three consecutive years in scoring?

117. Which Celtic is among the first four NBA players to average 25 points, seven rebounds, and seven assists in a single season?

118. Which two Celtics were on the NBA's 25th, 35th, and 50th anniversary teams?

119. Which Celtic was first to foul out of two All-Star games?

120. Who is the first Celtic to foul out of more than 90 games in his career?

121. Which Celtics rookie was first to play more than 3,000 minutes?

122. Who was the first member of the Celtics family to be honored with a commemorative black band on the left shoulder strap of the team jersey?

123. Name the Celtics executive who wrote a best-selling basketball book, titled *Basketball for the Player, the Fan and the Coach*.

124. Which Celtics player, when he retired, was one of the first three men in the NBA to make 1,000 or more career three-pointers?

125. Who were the first three Celtics coaches to win the NBA Coach of the Year award?

126. Which player ended up playing for the Celtics when the team owner drew his name out of a hat?

127. Which former Celtic was the first coach of the ABA's San Diego Conquistadors?

128. Which Celtic inspired a ballad containing the line, "Just a boy of 22, you made a name at LSU"?

129. Which Celtic's first appearance at Boston Garden prompted a fan to release a white dove?

130. Which Celtic was first to be a commissioner of a professional soccer league?

131. Who was the first Celtic to score 50 points in a playoff game?

132. Which Celtic was the first player to compete in NCAA and NBA Finals in back-to-back years?

133. Who was the first coach to capture NBA Coach of the Year honors with both the Cleveland Cavaliers and the Celtics?

134. Name the Celtic who was first to call Robert Parish "Chief"?

135. Which two Celtics were the first to release a basketball-related song?

136. The Celtics were the first Boston pro sports team to once have a former New York Yankees pitcher and a New York Giants defensive back as part owners. Can you name the two athletes?

137. The Celtics are one of only three teams from the NBA's first season still playing. What are the other two franchises?

138. Which three Celtics were first to reach 10,000 career rebounds?

139. Which Celtic was first to play more than 480 consecutive games for the team?

BOSTON BRUINS

1. Which one-time Bruin was the first NHL defenseman to lead his team in goals scored in a season?

2. Which Bruins coach was the first U.S.-born citizen to have been the MVP of a major pro hockey league?

3. Which Bruin was the first modern (post-1942) NHL player to play all six positions in a league game?

4. Which Bruin was the first defenseman to be named a first- or second-team All-Star 14 times?

5. Which Bruin was the first left wing to score more than 1,200 points in the NHL?

6. Which Bruin went undefeated in 32 consecutive games?

7. Which Bruins coach was the first in NHL history whose club had eleven 20-goal scorers?

8. Which one-time Bruin was the first defenseman with more than 310 career goals?

9. Which Bruin is the first NHL player to take more than 425 shots on goal in one season?

10. Which Bruin was the only 16-year-old to play in the NHL?

11. Which Bruins goalie allowed two goals in the first 24 seconds of a game?

12. Which one-time Bruin was the first player to score a goal in 10 consecutive playoff games?

13. Which Bruin was the first player with 10 penalties in one game?

14. Which Bruin was the first player with four assists in one period in an All-Star game?

15. What Bruins coach lost a Stanley Cup final in a game stopped in the second period by a power outage?

16. Which Bruin was the first defenseman to win a scoring title?

17. Which one-time Bruins goalie was the first to lead the NHL in goals against average seven times?

18. Name the Bruins coach who was the first coach with a season winning percentage over .830.

19. Which Bruins goalie, in a 1980 game against St. Louis, became the first goaltender to allow five goals in his only period of play in an NHL game?

20. Which one-time Bruin was the first NHL player with more than 100 points and 250 penalty minutes in the same season?

21. Which Bruin was the first African-American player in the NHL?

22. Who was the first to serve as player, coach, and general manager for the Bruins?

23. Who was the first man to serve four separate times as Bruins coach?

24. Who was the first Bruins team captain?

25. Who was the first Bruins player elected to the NHL Hall of Fame?

26. What Bruins line was first in NHL history to finish one-two-three in scoring for a season?

27. Which ex-Bruin was the first goalie to win 400 career games?

28. Which Bruins goalie was the first goaltender awarded an assist?

29. Which one-time Bruins goalie was the first NHL player to sign a WHA contract?

30. Can you name the one-time Bruin who was the first man to coach teams in the WHA and the Stanley Cup Finals?

31. Which one-time Bruin was the first teenager to captain an NHL team?

32. Which Bruins player was the first player to be penalized 2,000 minutes with one team during his career?

33. Which Bruin was the first player to compile 100 penalty minutes and 100 points in one season?

34. Which Bruin was the first hockey player to have a top-ten song written about him?

35. Which Bruin was the first non-Canadian-born 50-goal scorer in the NHL?

36. Name the Bruin who was the first rookie with 100 points who did not win the Calder Trophy as best rookie.

37. Which Bruin was the first player to sign a million-dollar contract?

38. Which one-time Bruin was the first player to use an aluminum-shafted stick?

39. Which Bruin was the first NHL player to wear a helmet?

40. What Bruins goalie was the first goaltender to decorate his mask?

41. Which Bruin was the first goaltender to use a blocker?

42. Which Bruins defenseman was the first to have his number retired?

43. The Bruins were the first team to put what on their uniforms?

44. Name the former Bruins star who was the first player to break one of Wayne Gretzky's 61 NHL records in regular-season play?

45. Which Bruin was the first player to play 20 NHL seasons?

46. Which Bruin was the first player inducted into the Hall of Fame without the mandatory three-year waiting period?

47. Which Bruins line was first to record 300 points in one season?

48. Which Bruin was the first player to compile 200 penalty minutes and finish among the top 10 scorers in the league for a season?

49. The Bruins and which opponent were the first two teams penalized 400 minutes in one game?

50. In 1970-71 the Bruins were the first team with two 50-goal scorers. Name the two players.

51. In a March 1991 game, what Quebec goalie, in a game against the Bruins, became the first goalie to face at least 70 shots and not lose?

52. What ex-Bruins goaltender was the first goalie to face two penalty shots in one game?

53. Can you name the Bruin who was the first NHL player convicted of vehicular homicide?

54. Which Bruins player was the first NHL player to receive a lifetime suspension for gambling?

55. Which Bruin was the first player to receive a lifetime suspension for assaulting a referee?

56. Which Bruin was the first player suspended for an entire calendar year for an on-ice incident?

57. Which Bruin was the first hockey player to be *Sports Illustrated*'s "Sportsman of the Year"?

58. The Boston Garden was the first NHL arena to award the visitors' penalty box to an opposition player. Who was the player?

59. Which Bruins coach was the first coach to pull his goalie for an extra attacker during a delayed penalty?

60. Which one-time Bruins coach was the first coach to win the Jack Adams trophy for best coach three times?

61. Which Bruin scored his 50th goal three times on his birthday?

62. Which Bruin was the first NHL player to score his 500th goal at age 40?

63. Which Bruin was the first scoring champion to record more assists than anyone else in the league had points in one season?

64. Which two Bruins were the first teammates to finish one-two in the league scoring race five times?

65. Which Bruin was the first player to win the same NHL trophy eight years in a row?

66. Which Bruin was the first defenseman to win four Hart Trophies as league MVP?

67. Which Bruin was the first player to have his Stanley Cup ring taken into space?

68. Which Bruin was the first player to appear in more than 200 playoff games before winning a Stanley Cup?

69. Which Bruin was the first player to score three overtime goals in one playoff year?

70. The 1970–71 Bruins set what dubious record?

71. Which one-time Bruins coach was the first ex-coach to get his name engraved on the Stanley Cup even though he was fired by the Cup-winning team in midseason?

72. Which Bruin was the first NHL player to win four individual trophies in one season?

73. Which one-time Bruin was the first NHL player to have 30 fighting majors in a season?

74. Who was the first Boston University alumnus to play for the Bruins?

75. In 1970–71 the Bruins were the first NHL team with four 100-point scorers in a single season. Can you name them?

76. Who coached the Bruins to their first Stanley Cup?

77. Who was the first American International College graduate to play for the Bruins?

78. Who were the first three members of the Bruins' 300-plus career goal club?

79. Who gave up Bobby Orr's first NHL goal?

80. Who was the first Bruins player of the 1950s to go on to play professional golf?

81. What was the name of Bobby Orr's first junior team?

82. Who was the first player in Bruins history to lead the team in goals, assists, points, and penalty minutes in the same season?

83. What team defeated the Bruins in their first Stanley Cup Finals appearance, in 1927?

84. Who were the first two players to share the TV-38 7th Player Award? (It began in 1968–69.)

85. Who was the first Bruin to win the league scoring title?

86. Which Bruin was first to win the MVP for Stanley Cup play more than once?

87. Which Bruin was the first NHL player to earn an annual salary of $100,000?

88. In 1997 who did Ray Bourque surpass to become first all-time in Bruins scoring?

89. Who was the first Bruins rookie to score four goals in a game?

90. Name the first Bruins rookie to score more than 90 points in a season.

91. Who were the first four Bruins goalies to be named NHL All-Stars by the Professional Hockey Writers' Association?

92. Who was the first Bruins non-goalie to both win the Calder Trophy (as Rookie of the Year) and be named first-team All-Star?

93. Who was the Bruins' first Rookie of the Year?

94. Who was the first Bruins coach to win a Stanley Cup in his rookie season?

95. Who was the first winner of the Bruins' 7th Player Award?

96. Who was the first defenseman to win the Bruins 7th Player Award?

97. Who were the first two Bruins to be first-team All-Stars at a wing?

98. Who was the first Bruin to win three Lady Byng Trophies (for sportsmanship and gentlemanly conduct, combined with performance in play)?

99. What short-term Bruin was the first American to win the Conn Smythe Trophy as playoff MVP?

100. Which Bruin was the first non–Montreal Canadian to score two Stanley Cup–winning goals?

101. Which Bruin was a member of the 1980 U.S. Olympic hockey team?

102. After Phil Esposito was traded to the Rangers, who was the first Bruin to score more than 50 goals in a season?

103. Name the Bruin who was the first professional athlete indicted for a crime committed during a game.

104. Which Bruin was the first NHL player to score three shorthanded goals in one playoff season?

105. Which one-time Bruin was the first NHL player to have 50 goals, 100 points, and 200 penalty minutes in the same season?

106. Which one-time Bruins goalie was the first player to win a Canada Cup, a Stanley Cup, and a World Championship?

107. Who were the first two Bruins to wear uniform number 13?

108. Which Bruin was first to score his 50th goal for a season in the month of February?

109. Which one-time Bruin was awarded the first penalty shot in the overtime of a Stanley Cup game?

110. The Bruins qualified for the playoffs in how many consecutive years?

111. Which two 2006 Bruins were first-team Division 1 Hockey All-Americans in 2004–05?

112. Who was the Bruins' first NHL All-Star game MVP since Ray Bourque in 1996?

113. Who was the first Bruin since Bobby Orr in 1975 to lead the NHL in assists?

114. Who was the first Bruins goalie since Frankie Brimsek in 1942 to lead the NHL in goals-against average?

115. Who was the first Bruin to lead the NHL in penalty minutes?

116. Who was the first Bruin to win the Lady Byng Trophy?

117. Who was the first Bruin to win the Frank Selke Trophy as outstanding defensive forward?

118. Who was the first Bruins coach to win the Jack Adams Award as the NHL's best coach?

119. Who was the first Bruins coach to be inducted into the U.S. Hockey Hall of Fame as a player?

120. Who was the first Bruin to be a member of both the Hockey Hall of Fame and the U.S. Hockey Hall of Fame as a player?

121. Which goalie, who played a portion of his career with the Bruins, was first to have more than 100 shutouts in a career?

122. Who was the first Bruin with more than 300 penalty minutes in one season?

123. One player scored 10 points in an NHL game against the Bruins. Who was he?

124. Who were the first two Bruins to share the team captaincy?

125. Who was the first Bruin to be team captain for longer than 10 years?

126. Which Bruins coach was voted first in a list of Massachusetts high school hockey players in a *Sports Illustrated* poll?

127. Which two players, each with only one good eye, were signed by the Bruins?

128. Which Bruins rookie goalie was the first to allow only one goal in a seven-game span?

129. Name the former Bruin who was an NHL scout killed on United Airlines Flight 175 on September 11, 2001?

130. Which Bruin wore number 2, the first number retired by the team?

131. Which Bruins star left the team during World War II to serve for three years in Canada's Royal Canadian air force?

132. Which Bruin was the first to score 50 goals in a season when he was at least 35 years old?

133. What was Joe Thornton's first number when he joined the Bruins?

134. On December 4, 1982, who scored the first Bruins hat trick in Montreal since 1959?

135. Who was the first Czech-born player to play for the Bruins?

136. What was the nickname given to one-time Bruins and Canadiens enforcer Chris Nilan?

137. Name the defenseman traded to the Bruins in late 1977–78 who became the first NHL player to play for four teams in one season.

138. Which one-time Bruins defenseman was the first U.S.-born player to play in 1,000 career games in the NHL?

139. Which Bruin was the first player ever to win a gold medal at the World Senior Championships, in 2004, and a gold medal at the World Junior Championships, in 2005? (He played for Canada.)

140. From 1998 to 2001 the Bruins roster included the first player picked in the 1997 draft and also the final player picked. Can you name the two players?

141. Which Bruin was the first player in NHL history to have 100 assists in one season?

142. Which Bruins star was first to have his younger brother chosen by the team in the NHL entry draft?

143. In what season did the Bruins become the first NHL team ever to win 50 games in one year?

144. Which Bruin was the first defenseman in NHL history to score a combined 20 goals with two different teams in a single season?

145. The first brother-against-brother goal in NHL history was scored against which famous Bruins goaltender in 1937?

146. Which Bruins coach was the first rookie coach in NHL history to win at least 55 games in a season?

147. Who was the first player to win three Stanley Cups with the Bruins?

148. Which Bruin was the first defenseman in modern NHL history to score a hat trick in a playoff game?

149. Which one-time Bruin was the first player to be traded during a season and compile 100-plus points during that season?

150. Who were the first two Bruins to lead the team in scoring for six seasons?

151. Who were the first four players in Bruins history to lead the team in penalty minutes and points in a season?

152. Since 2000, who were the first two Bruins to be selected to the NHL's All-Rookie team?

153. In 2003 which Bruin was the first player in NHL history to score two goals in the first 27 seconds of a game?

154. Which Bruin had a hat trick in the first regular-season game at the Fleet Center?

155. In Bobby Orr's first NHL All-Star game in 1968, what uniform number did he wear?

156. Which two Bruins were first to have more than one 50-goal season for the team?

157. Can you name the first four Bruins to record seven points in one game?

158. Which Bruins player scored six consecutive goals for the team over three games, January 29–February 1, 2004?

159. Who was the first Bruin born in the former Yugoslavia?

160. Who was the first Bruin born in the state of Virginia?

161. Who was the first Polish-born Bruins player?

162. Which Bruin scored the first regular-season goal at the Fleet Center?

163. Which Bruins goaltender recorded the first regular-season shutout at the Fleet Center?

164. Which Bruin is the NHL's all-time leader in wins and shutouts for a goaltender born in England?

165. Bruins great Gerry Cheevers was first the property of which NHL team?

166. In October 1978 the Bruins traded goalie Ron Grahame to Los Angeles for a first-round choice that was used to select what future star?

167. In 1998–99 which player became the first Bruins goaltender to reach double digits in shutouts for a season since Frank Brimsek in 1938–39?

168. Which goalie in 1960 became the first Bruins goaltender to wear a mask?

169. Who were the first brothers to play in the same season for the Bruins?

170. Who were the first two Boston University goaltenders to play for the Bruins?

171. Which NY Islanders defenseman won the 1976 Norris Trophy as the NHL's top defenseman, the first person other than Bobby Orr to win it in nine years?

172. Where did the Bruins play in their first four seasons?

173. Which Bruin was the first goalie in NHL history to record three consecutive home-ice shutouts in the playoffs?

174. Who was the first Bruin to score a point in 22 consecutive games?

175. Which Bruin wrestled an eight-foot-tall brown bear?

176. By what name was the Boston Garden known when it was built in 1927?

177. Which Bruins coach worked as a police officer for 17 years?

178. Name the Bruin who wore both Eddie Shore's number 2 and Bobby Orr's number 4 during his tenure with the team.

179. Which son of a famous Bruin won the Bruins' 7th Player Award in 1991?

180. Who was the first member of the Tuscarora American Indian tribe to become a Bruin?

181. At the September 26, 1995, celebration of the closing of the Boston Garden, what three Bruins were first asked to have their picture taken together in the penalty box?

182. Which Bruin had a pitcher of beer dumped over his head by a Boston mayor?

183. Who was the first Bruin to bean an opposing fan with his own shoe during a brawl in the stands?

184. Which Bruin was the son of an NFL quarterback?

185. Name the first two Bruins stars of "The Big Bad Bruins" teams of the late 1960s and early 1970s who had fought one another in an exhibition game at the Boston Garden in 1965.

186. From which Bruins player did singer René Rancourt, who sang the national anthem for the Bruins, copy his signature "fist pump" seen at the conclusion of the song?

187. Which Bruin was the first to have his own Boston-area TV talk show?

188. Which Bruin was the first to appear in an X-rated movie?

189. Which four Bruins defensemen of the early 1970s were referred to by a group name that echoed the title of a popular movie?

RED SOX ANSWERS

1. Jackie Jensen, in the Rose Bowl with the University of California and in the World Series with the New York Yankees
2. Dennis Eckersley, with the Oakland A's
3. Mark "The Bird" Fidrych, when he was with the Detroit Tigers
4. Tracy Stallard to Roger Maris, in a Red Sox–Yankees game
5. Tim Wakefield, 172 pitches in 1993
6. Billy Conigliaro in 1969 and Mike Greenwell in 1985
7. Dennis Eckersley
8. Luis Tiant and Bobby Ojeda
9. Ellis Burks, in 1987
10. Rick Wise won an All-Star game in 1973 while with the St. Louis Cardinals, and both an ALCS and a World Series game in 1975 while with the Red Sox.
11. Jim Rice, DH and OF
12. Joe Cronin, player-manager in 1943
13. Ted Williams
14. Nomar Garciaparra
15. Ray Culp, from 1968 to 1972
16. Bill Campbell in 1977, Tom Gordon in 1998, and Derek Lowe in 2000
17. Ted Williams, on July 4, 1948, vs. Philadelphia A's
18. Scott Hatteberg, on August 6, 2001
19. Ted Williams, in 1957
20. Ken Harrelson, on June 14, 1968, vs. Cleveland
21. Cy Young, Roger Clemens, and Tim Wakefield
22. Babe Ruth, in 1918
23. Wade Boggs, 1985–1991
24. Pete Runnels, in 1960, batted .320 with 35 RBIs
25. Jason Varitek
26. Mike Timlin

27. Carl Yastrzemski (1969–70) and David Ortiz (2004–05)
28. Jeff Russell, in 1993
29. Johnny Pesky and Marty Barrett
30. Bill Buckner, 673 at bats in 1985
31. Don Schwall in 1961 and Jonathan Papelbon in 2006
32. Carl Yastrzemski, 190
33. David Ortiz, in 2006
34. Felix Mantilla, in 1965
35. Walt Dropo and Bobby Doerr, in 1950
36. Harry Hooper, who won the World Series with the Red Sox in 1912, 1915, 1916, and 1918
37. Bill Buckner, in 1982 with the Cubs and in 1985 with the Red Sox
38. Tommy Harper, with the Milwaukee Brewers, 31 home runs and 38 steals in 1970
39. Billy Goodman, who played first, second, and third base, shortstop, and left field in 1950
40. The playing of the national anthem
41. Johnny Pesky, May 8, 1946
42. Trot Nixon, June 10, 2003, vs. St. Louis
43. Jim Lonborg. The photo of Sam "Mayday" Malone in *Cheers* was of Jim Lonborg in uniform.
44. Babe Ruth. Jack Webb, who played Sgt. Joe Friday on *Dragnet*, wore badge #714, a tribute to Ruth's career home-run total. In reruns the show was called *Badge 714*.
45. A photo of Babe Ruth, carried by a 39-year-old Sox fan, in an attempt to exorcise the "Curse of the Bambino"
46. Curt Schilling, while with the Arizona Diamondbacks
47. Bob Stanley, in 1980
48. Pete Runnels, in 1960, at first base and second base
49. Doug Mirabelli
50. Gary Allenson, Rich Gedman, and Scott Hatteberg
51. Eric Hinske and Mark Loretta, in 2006, vs. Yankees
52. Derek Lowe
53. Spike Owen
54. Mike Cubbage, third-base coach
55. Matt Young lost 2-1 to Cleveland, April 12, 1992.
56. Chuck Schilling
57. Mildred "Babe" Didrikson Zaharias, considered the greatest female athlete of all time
58. Luis Aparicio and Orlando Cepeda
59. Bill Lee, in 1978
60. George Scott, in 1966
61. Wade Boggs
62. Tim Wakefield, in 1999

63. Jackie Jensen, in 1956
64. Ted Williams, in 1940
65. Lou Gehrig, with the Yankees in June 1927
66. Babe Ruth and Mickey Mantle
67. Derek Sanderson Jeter
68. Ellis Burks in 1987 and Bob Zupcic in 1992
69. Jimmy Foxx, in 1932 with the Philadelphia Athletics
70. Carl Everett
71. Abe Alvarez
72. Tony Conigliaro in 1965 and Bronson Arroyo in 2005
73. Dale Sveum, in 2004
74. Jim Pagliaroni, in 1955
75. Jimmy Foxx, in 1940
76. Carl Yastrzemski
77. Carl Yastrzemski, in 1963
78. David Ortiz, "The Big Papi," Delta Airlines
79. Cy Young, 1903
80. Curtis Pride, 1997
81. Wade Boggs, 1986–1988. The other player is Lou Gehrig.
82. Carlton Fisk, in 1977
83. Reggie Cleveland, in 1975
84. Marty Barrett, in 1992
85. Derek Lowe
86. Joe Morgan
87. Ugueth Urbina, in Venezuela. In early 2007 the case was still awaiting resolution.
88. Juan Marichal
89. Don Aase. David Aardsma broke in with the San Francisco Giants in 2004.
90. Babe Ruth
91. Reggie Smith, in 1970
92. Rudy York, with the Detroit Tigers in 1938
93. Jimmy Foxx, in 1932 for the Philadelphia A's
94. Ellis Burks completed the feat while with the San Francisco Giants in 1998.
95. Tom Yawkey, Red Sox owner 1933–1976
96. Harry Hooper, in 1913
97. Edgar Renteria, from St. Louis to Boston, 2004–2005
98. Don Baylor
99. Babe Ruth in 1917, and Pedro Martinez in 2000
100. Tony Armas, in 1984
101. Dick Williams
102. Vic Wertz, in 1960, with 103 RBIs and 45 runs scored
103. Don Baylor, in 1979 with the California Angels
104. Curt Schilling, with Randy Johnson for Arizona in 2002
105. Harry Hooper, in 1915

106. Jose Canseco, born in Cuba
107. Derek Lowe saved 42 games in 2000.
108. Leslie Sterling, in 1994
109. Earl Wilson, June 26, 1962, against the California Angels
110. Doug Griffin, 1992
111. Johnny Pesky, "The Pesky Pole" at Fenway Park
112. Eldon Auker, in 1939
113. The Hall of Famers were Jimmie Foxx, Ted Williams, and Joe Cronin. The fourth player was Jim Tabor.
114. Tony Pena, for the Kansas City Royals, vs. Luis Pujols of the Detroit Tigers
115. Tim Wakefield, August 8, 2004, vs. Detroit Tigers. The Red Sox won.
116. Dale Alexander, 1932
117. Williams
118. Roger Clemens
119. Harvard College
120. Woodrow Wilson, in 1915 when the Red Sox played the Phillies
121. 1931
122. Walt Dropo, 1950
123. Luis Tiant, April 6, 1973
124. Jeff Reardon, in 1985 for Montreal and in 1988 for Minnesota
125. Juan Marichal, on June 15, 1963, while pitching for San Francisco
126. Dennis Eckersley
127. Josh Beckett, on August 8, 2006, vs. New York Yankees
128. Orlando Cepeda, in 1973
129. Don Baylor, with the Colorado Rockies in 1995
130. Tony Pena, with the Kansas City Royals in 2003
131. Tom Seaver
132. Ken "Hawk" Harrelson
133. Mascot "Wally the Green Monster"
134. Wil Cordero
135. Billy Martin, in 1950
136. Bobby Doerr
137. David Ortiz. The others were Sandy Alomar Jr. and Barry Bonds.
138. Jim Lonborg, 1967
139. Ted Williams
140. Jeff Bagwell, traded to the Houston Astros in 1990
141. Luis Aparicio
142. The Pilgrims
143. The Pittsburgh Pirates
144. Cy Young had 749 complete games from 1890 to 1911, including 283 with the Red Sox. Second place (616) is held by James "Pud" Galvin, who pitched for Buffalo, Pittsburg, and St. Louis between 1879 and 1892.
145. Tris Speaker, Hall of Famer
146. 1907, when the owner changed the name from Pilgrims

147. Hugh Bradley, for the Red Sox. It was his only home run in the 1912 season.
148. Babe Ruth
149. Eddie Collins, in 1933
150. Robert
151. Hanley Ramirez, Florida Marlins, 2006
152. Harry Hooper
153. Red Ruffing
154. Frank Malzone, in 1957
155. Carroll Hardy, in 1960
156. Dick "The Monster" Radatz; 6 feet, 6 inches; 280 pounds
157. Elston Howard
158. Americo
159. Don "Popeye" Zimmer
160. Nick Esasky retired in 1990.
161. John Kennedy, in 1970
162. Luis Arroyo, 1961
163. 1946
164. Jim Tabor (1939) and Rudy York (1946)
165. Jimmy Foxx, with the Philadelphia A's in 1932 and 1933, and the Red Sox in 1938
166. Joe Cronin managed 2,007 games.
167. Pitcher Wes and catcher Rick Ferrell, from 1934 to 1937
168. July 14, 1946, by the Cleveland Indians
169. Harry Hooper
170. Cy Young (1901), Tex Hughson (1942), and Jim Lonborg (1967)
171. Mike "Pinky" Higgins, in 1938
172. Bill Dineen in 1903 and "Smoky" Joe Wood in 1912
173. Jackie Jensen, for the University of California
174. Harry Hooper
175. Jackie Robinson, Sam Jethroe, and Marvin Williams
176. Dick Radatz, 104
177. Tufts University, Medford, Massachusetts
178. "Smoky" Joe Wood and Joe Wood Jr., and Ed Connolly and Ed Connolly Jr.
179. Al Benton
180. Gerry O'Leary
181. Charles Stahl in 1906 and Garland Stahl in 1912–1913
182. Herb Score, Cleveland Indians
183. Earl Wilson, June 26, 1962
184. Lou Criger and Bill Carrigan
185. Tom Doran, from 1904 to 1906
186. Bill Monboquette, 1963, and Jim Lonborg, 1967
187. Ben Chapman
188. At Wrigley Field in Los Angeles vs. the Los Angeles Angels, off Jerry Casale, May 9, 1961.

189. Black
190. Charlottesville, Virginia
191. "Smoky" Joe Wood and Babe Ruth
192. Bill Campbell
193. Rico Petrocelli, 40 in 1969
194. Buck Freeman
195. Johnny Pesky, in 1942, 1946, and 1947
196. Shortstop
197. Ernie Shore. In 1917 he replaced Babe Ruth, who was ejected after the game's first batter.
198. Ted Cox, in 1977
199. Frank Malzone, 1957–1959
200. Dick Radatz struck out 181 in 1964
201. Dick Stuart, first base, 1958–1964. His nickname was "Dr. Strangeglove."
202. Cy Young, in 1908
203. Jackie Jensen, retired 1960
204. Carlton Fisk
205. Dom Dimaggio
206. Tom Gordon, in Stephen King's *The Girl Who Loved Tom Gordon*
207. Bowling. The alley under Fenway Park was closed in October 2004 to make way for new team offices.
208. Hideo Nomo
209. Jerry Remy, on June 14, 1980
210. Terry Francona, in 1994
211. "Lefty" Grove and Cy Young
212. 1936
213. Everett Scott played 1,093; Rick Burleson played 1,004.
214. Bob Stanley
215. Carlton Fisk, in 1972
216. Mel Parnell, 123 career wins
217. Joe Cronin, American League president, 1959–1973
218. Ted Williams. The others were Tim Raines and Ricky Henderson.
219. Carl Yastrzemski
220. Carney Lansford and Dwight Evans
221. Eddie Bressoud, in 1964
222. Mark Bellhorn, in 2002
223. Wade Boggs
224. Jeff Reardon, 9 in 49 chances in 1991
225. Doug Mirabelli, through 2006
226. Carl Yastrzemski
227. Dick Stuart
228. Glenn Hoffman
229. Bruce Hurst
230. Rudy York (1946), Norm Zauchin (1955), and Fred Lynn (1975)

231. Earl Wilson, 21 in 1963
232. Dom DiMaggio
233. David McCarty, in the 12th inning of the July 1, 2004, game vs. the New York Yankees. He played pitcher, first base, and the three outfield positions.
234. Carl Yastrzemski (1967) and Rico Petrocelli (1969)
235. Fred Lynn, in 1979
236. Ted Williams
237. Wade Boggs, in 1985
238. Mike Torrez
239. Tony Conigliaro
240. Mike Greenwell
241. Babe Ruth, "Lefty" Grove, Mel Parnell, and Rogelio Moret
242. Trot Nixon
243. Dalton Jones
244. Skip Lockwood
245. "Smoky" Joe Wood won 34 in 1912.
246. Harry Agganis
247. Fred Lynn
248. Dennis "Oil Can" Boyd
249. Ted Williams (1939), Fred Lynn (1975), and Brian Daubach (1999)
250. Fred Lynn, Jim Rice, and Carl Yastrzemski, in 1975
251. Jose Santiago, 1967 World Series
252. Derek Lowe, in 1999
253. Dwight Evans
254. Bernie Carbo, in 1975
255. Cy Young, in 1903
256. Roger Clemens, in 1986
257. Rick Wise. The other was Jim Bunning.
258. Every regular on the team, including the manager and coaches, was obtained from other Major League clubs.
259. Jin Ho Cho, on July 4, 1998
260. John Wyatt, on July 6, 1966
261. Trot Nixon, on July 15, 2004
262. Roger Clemens, in 1986
263. Tony Conigliaro, at age 22, in 1967
264. Dave Stapleton and Sam Horn
265. Billy Hatcher
266. Tom Burgmeier
267. Troy O'Leary, August 2, 2001; and Nomar Garciaparra, July 3, 2002
268. Charlie Sheen
269. Jimmy Foxx, Ted Williams, and Jim Rice
270. Don Baylor, in 1986
271. Bob Stanley, in August 1980
272. Johnny Pesky, in August 1946

273. Ferguson Jenkins
274. Al Nipper
275. Tim Wakefield, in 1996
276. Bob Watson
277. Butch Hobson, 162 strikeouts in 1977
278. Calvin Pickering
279. Roger Clemens, at the celebration of the American League East–clinching win in 1995
280. Diego Segui, in 1974
281. Tony Armas batted only .218 while driving in 107 runs in 1983.
282. Ted Williams. "The Ted Williams Bill" would have levied a fine of $50 on a person who uttered "profane or slanderous statements at participants in sporting events." It did not pass!
283. Babe Ruth's
284. Don Zimmer
285. Nomar Garciaparra, .372 in 2000
286. John Valentin, 101 in 1985
287. Mike Greenwell, in 1988
288. Carl Yastrzemski, Yaz Bread
289. Ken Brett, in 1967
290. Bobby Doerr, in 1944
291. Jimmie Foxx
292. Ted Williams
293. Baseball clown Al Schacht
294. Ted Williams, the Ted Williams Tunnel in Boston
295. Jim Lonborg, in 1967
296. Mike "Pinky" Higgins pleaded guilty to negligent homicide in a death caused by his car and was sentenced to four years at hard labor.
297. Tony Conigliaro
298. New York Yankees
299. Sherm Feller, "Summertime, Summertime"
300. John Burkett, in ten-pin bowling!
301. Ray Culp
302. Mark Bellhorn, in 2004
303. The landing point of a 502-foot home run hit by Ted Williams in June 1946
304. Greg Harris
305. John Olerud
306. Wade Boggs
307. Wendell Kim, third-base coach
308. Jimmy Piersall, to celebrate his 100th career home run
309. Roger Clemens, with New York Yankees
310. Sparky Lyle
311. Dick Williams
312. Ralph Houk, with the Yankees

313. Ferguson Jenkins
314. Dick Stuart, in 1969
315. Don Zimmer, in 1962
316. Mike Greenwell had nine RBIs in a 9-8 win over Seattle in 1996.
317. Derek Lowe, in 2004
318. Andre Dawson
319. Jimmie Foxx
320. Jimmie Foxx's 50 home runs in 1938 were second to Hank Greenberg's 58.
321. Johnny Pesky led in 1942, served three years in the military, then led again in 1946 and 1947.
322. Carl Yastrzemski
323. Matt Stairs, for Oakland from 1997 to 2000
324. Jackie Jensen, Carl Yastrzemski, Ellis Burks, John Valentin, and Nomar Garciaparra
325. David Ortiz, in 2004
326. Dom DiMaggio, 15 steals in 1950, 100 in his career
327. Butch Hobson
328. Tris Speaker, Harry Hooper, and Johnny Damon
329. Pete Runnels, in 1966, for 16 games
330. Pumpsie Green, Earl Wilson, and Willie Tasby
331. Derek Lowe. The other was Craig Lefferts.
332. Babe Ruth, "Lefty" Grove, Wes Farrell, and Ellis Kinder
333. Bill Mueller, in 2003
334. Jackie Jensen, playing for the University of California in 1948
335. Clyde Vollmer and Ted Williams
336. The sinking of the *Titanic*
337. Rolando Arrojo, for Tampa Bay in 1998
338. Dwight Evans, off Jack Morris in 1986 at Detroit
339. Jim Rice, in 1978
340. Ted Williams and Jackie Jensen
341. Jimmy Foxx, Bobby Doerr, Joe Cronin, and Jim Tabor, in 1940
342. Cy Young and Pedro Martinez
343. Roger Clemens
344. Nomar Garciaparra. The other is Tom Brady.
345. Don Baylor
346. Tony Cloninger, in 1966, for Atlanta. He was a pitcher!
347. Jackie Jensen, in 1958
348. Walt Dropo, in 1950
349. Elston Howard
350. Josh Beckett, in 2003, with Florida. The other two were Johnny Podres (Brooklyn, 1955) and Lew Burdette (Milwaukee, 1957).
351. Carlton Fisk (1975), Trot Nixon (2003), and David Ortiz (2004)
352. Bret Saberhagen, for the New York Mets, in 1994, had a 14-4 record in 127 innings with only 13 walks.

353. Elston Howard, who early in his career played behind Yogi Berra with the New York Yankees
354. Babe Ruth, in 1919, the Louisville Slugger bat
355. Jim Lonborg, in 1967 vs. St. Louis, a one-hitter and a three-hitter
356. Mike Boddicker, in 1990
357. Cecil Cooper, in June 1974
358. Wade Boggs. The other was Ty Cobb.
359. Mike Benjamin, for the Giants in 1995
360. Luis Aparicio, 2,581 games at shortstop
361. Don Zimmer. The others were Leo Durocher, Casey Stengel, and Frank Robinson.
362. Luis Aparicio, in 1984
363. "Smoky" Joe Wood pitched for the Red Sox in 1912 and played outfield for the Cleveland Indians in 1920.
364. Manager Terry Francona. He and his father, Tito, played for 13 teams: Tito for nine and Terry for four.
365. Carl Yastrzemski, in *The Shining*. Jack Nicholson swung the bat at Shelley Duvall's character.
366. Mark Whitten. For the St. Louis Cardinals in a doubleheader in 1993, he hit 4 home runs in one game, had 12 RBIs in one game, and had 13 RBIs for the doubleheader.
367. Curt Schilling. The other is Tiger Woods.
368. Jimmie Foxx. Jimmy Dugan, Tom Hanks's character in *A League of Their Own*, was based on Foxx, who once managed in the All-American Girls Professional Baseball League.
369. Frank Malzone of the Red Sox won 3 of the first 19 Gold Gloves at third base. Brooks Robinson of the Baltimore Orioles won the other 16.
370. Jimmy Piersall
371. Tris Speaker
372. John Wyatt, in 1964 for the Kansas City A's
373. Carlton Fisk. The others were Rick Dempsey and Nolan Ryan.
374. Wilbur Wood, Dennis Eckersley, and Derek Lowe
375. Gene Conley, for the Boston Red Sox, Celtics, and Bruins
376. Reggie Smith. The others are Chili Davis and Eddie Murray.
377. Jeff Reardon, for the Expos in 1986, the Twins in 1987, and the Red Sox in 1991
378. Ferguson Jenkins. The others were Catfish Hunter and Rollie Fingers.
379. Reggie Smith. The other is Frank Robinson.
380. "Lefty" Grove
381. Orlando Cepeda, for the St. Louis Cardinals in 1967
382. Juan Marichal
383. Babe Ruth. While making the movie *Headin' Home*, he arrived late at the ballpark and didn't have time to remove his makeup before taking the field.

PATRIOTS ANSWERS

1. Jim Nance, in 1966
2. Tully Banta-Cain, cousin to Jeff Leonard and Rodney Rogers
3. Troy Brown
4. Troy Brown, with Deion Sanders and Roy Green
5. Bob Dee, in 1961
6. Julius Adams, Tony McGee, and Mike Hawkins
7. Raymond Clayborn, in 1977
8. Jim Nance, Sam Cunningham, and Tony Collins
9. Prentice McCray, in 1976 vs. New York Jets
10. Steve Nelson
11. Garin Veris, 10.5 sacks in 1985
12. Curtis Martin, scored 18 points in 1997 vs. Pittsburgh
13. Jack Concannon, from Boston College
14. Mike Haynes, in 1976
15. Rodney Harrison
16. Mike Vrabel, on December 26, 2005
17. Lonie Paxton, on A&E's *Inked*
18. Tony Franklin, kicking for Texas A&M against Baylor, October 16, 1976
19. Raymond Clayborn
20. Curtis Martin, in 1996
21. Robert Edwards
22. Ben Coates, 1992–1996
23. Sam Cunningham and Curtis Martin
24. Larry Garron (1963) and Stanley Morgan (1986)
25. Babe Parilli, in 1963
26. Larry Garron, in 1961
27. Tom Tupa, in 1997

28. Raymond Clayborn, three in 1977; and Kevin Faulk, two in 2002
29. Rodney Harrison, in 1997, for the San Diego Chargers
30. Christian Fauria, in 2002, vs. Pittsburgh
31. Andre Tippett, 100 career sacks; Julius Adams, 79.5; and Tony McGee, 72.5
32. John Smith, Tony Franklin, and Adam Vinatieri
33. Mike Vrabel, in 2003, with a TD pass from Tom Brady
34. Lisa Olson, with player Zeke Mowatt, who allegedly exposed himself to her
35. Joe Bellino, John Huarte, Jim Plunkett, and Doug Flutie
36. Jim Colclough and Michael Timpson
37. Ron Burton, 91 yards, in 1962 vs. Denver
38. Babe Parilli, who did it twice (November 15, 1964, and October 15, 1967), and Steve Grogan (September 9, 1979)
39. Irving Fryar
40. Mark Henderson, the inmate who snowplowed a clear spot to allow John Smith to kick the winning field goal in a 3–0 victory over Miami in 1982
41. Steve Grogan
42. Randy Vataha
43. Babe Parilli, in 1964
44. Victor Kiam, who owned Remington Products
45. Troy Brown, in 2002, vs. Kansas City
46. Tedy Bruschi, in 2000–2003
47. Troy Brown and Terry Glenn, in 2000
48. Harvard Stadium, in 1960
49. Jim Plunkett, a Heisman winner at Stanford, the Patriots' first draft pick in 1971, and a Super Bowl winner with Oakland in 1981
50. Stanley Morgan, Terry Glenn, and Troy Brown
51. Mike Haynes, Irving Fryar, and Troy Brown
52. Terrell Buckley, in 2002
53. Corey Dillon, who did it both times with the Cincinnati Bengals
54. Troy Brown, in 2000, 2001, and 2002
55. Mack Herron, 14.8 yards in 1974
56. Tedy Bruschi
57. Tom Tupa, averaged 44.7 yards
58. Tony Collins, 212 yards, in 1983
59. Gino Cappelletti, on December 18, 1965. A receiver and a placekicker, Capelletti scored four touchdowns and kicked four extra points.
60. Stephen Neal
61. Corey Dillon
62. Patrick Pass
63. Mike Haynes, four in four years; and Russ Francis, three in four years
64. Charley Gogolak, in 1971
65. Mack Herron, Stephen Starring, Derrick Cullors, and Bethel Johnson
66. Babe Parilli, in 1967
67. 65 years, since 1941

68. Lonie Paxton
69. Stephen Neal
70. Tom Brady attended the same high school as Lynn Swann and Barry Bonds.
71. Corey Dillon, with 246 yards in a game for the Cincinnati Bengals, 1997
72. Curtis Martin, in 1997, vs. New York Jets
73. Marty Schottenheimer
74. Logan Mankins
75. Robert Edwards
76. Larry Garron, ran for 116 yards in 10 carries, in 1961, vs. Buffalo
77. Jim Colclough, in 1962
78. Jim Plunkett, 1971
79. Larry Garron, in 1961
80. Mosi Tatupu, in 1986
81. Dave Meggett, in 1996
82. Jim Colclough. Michael Timpson and Daniel Graham have done it since.
83. Tony Eason, in 1996
84. Tony Collins, Leroy Thompson, and Kevin Faulk
85. Don Blackmon, in 1985
86. Oakland Raiders, with a score of 20–6
87. Allen Carter, averaged 27.2 yards, in 1975–76
88. Andre Tippett, five times, 1984–1988
89. Bruce Armstrong played in 212 games, Julius Adams in 206.
90. Irving Fryar, in Super Bowl XX
91. New Jersey Generals of the USFL
92. 1991
93. Drew Bledsoe, in 1994, vs. Minnesota
94. Larry Garron, in 1961, vs. Buffalo
95. Cornerback
96. Steve Nelson, with 207 tackles in 1984
97. Ron Burton, 127 yards, in 1960, vs. Denver
98. Terry Glenn, 214 yards, in 1999, vs. Cleveland
99. Dick Christy, 124 yards, in 1960, vs. Oakland
100. Mike Haynes, 89 yards, in 1976, vs. Buffalo
101. Steve Grogan, 1975–1990
102. Bill Belichick, with Mike Ditka
103. 20 games
104. Art Graham, 51 catches in 1966
105. Nick Buoniconti, 1963–1967
106. John Hannah, offensive lineman
107. John Hannah
108. Tony Eason, in a 31–14 win over Miami in the 1985 AFC Championship game
109. Tom Yewcic, 68 yards in the 1968 AFL Championship game vs. San Diego. The Patriots lost 51-10.

110. Steve Nelson
111. Raymond Clayborn, 47 yards, in 1978, vs. Houston
112. Miami won 29-28 after trailing 14-10 at the half.
113. Andre Tippett, in 1993
114. Maurice Hurst
115. Sam Cunningham and Tony Collins
116. Carl Garrett, with 29 catches in 1969
117. Todd Collins, 40 yards, in a 1997 wild-card game vs. Miami
118. Howard Cosell
119. Rohan Davey
120. The 1978 team
121. Richard Seymour
122. Scott Secules
123. Ron Meyer
124. Irving Fryar, wide receiver
125. Cornerback Assante Samuel, in week 14, 34 yards, vs. Cincinnati
126. Harold Jackson, who also played for four other teams
127. Steve Grogan
128. Stanley Morgan
129. John Hannah
130. Quarterback Harvey White, in December 1959
131. 31 years
132. Pittsburgh Steelers, won 34-20
133. Jim Nance, rushed 1,458 yards in 1966
134. William Sullivan, Victor Kiam, James Orthwein, and Robert Kraft (the only four owners)
135. Roman Phifer, named for Rams quarterback Roman Gabriel
136. Corey Dillon, in the 2004 AFC Division Playoffs in a 20-3 win over the Indianapolis Colts
137. Raymond Berry, in 1986
138. Denver Broncos
139. Leonard Russell
140. Dan Klecko. His father, Joe, played for the New York Jets.
141. Craig James, 104 and 105 yards in 1986
142. Tom Brady and David Patten, 91 yards, on October 21, 2001
143. Curtis Martin, with a 78-yard touchdown run vs. Pittsburgh in January 1997
144. Gino Cappelletti, with four in 1960. He tied with Harry Jacobs.
145. Carl Garrett, averaged 15.5 yards in 1971
146. Tom Brady, as a catcher
147. Matt Cassel, who played for Northridge, California in 1994
148. Laurence Maroney, with Marion Barber, Minnesota in 2003–2004
149. Troy Brown
150. Deion Branch

151. Logan Mankins, in 2005
152. September 16, 1960, 28-24 over the New York Titans
153. Gino Cappelletti
154. Bob Gallagher
155. Bobby Leo, in 1967–68
156. Justin Canale, 1965–1968, and Whit Canale, 1968
157. Joe Kapp
158. John Hannah
159. Bob Dee, defensive end
160. At the University of Massachusetts, Amherst
161. Jim Colclough, September 9, 1960
162. Schaefer Stadium, home of the New England Patriots, 1971–1982
163. Kevin Faulk, in 2002
164. Adam Vinatieri and Curtis Martin, both in 1996
165. Jon Vaughn, in 1992
166. Julius Adams, in 1977
167. Jim Plunkett, who attempted 46 passes with no interceptions in two Super Bowls with the Oakland Raiders, 1981 and 1984
168. Laurence Maroney, in October 2006, vs. Cincinnati
169. Joe Bellino
170. Joe Kapp, who played in the Rose Bowl with the University of California, the Grey Cup with the B.C. Lions, and the Super Bowl with the Minnesota Vikings
171. Doug Flutie, for Flutie Flakes cereal
172. Bill Parcells coached the New York Giants and the Patriots to Super Bowls. The other four were Don Shula, Dan Reeves, Dick Vermeil, and Mike Holmgren.
173. Adam Vinatieri. The other is Jason Elam.
174. Doug Flutie, threw 368 touchdown passes
175. Drew Bledsoe. The other three are Craig Morton, Jim Kelly, and Kerry Collins.
176. Joe Kapp
177. Steve Grogan
178. 2003, 12-0 including preseason, regular season, and postseason
179. 1994
180. 1996 and 1997
181. Dante Scarnecchia, assistant head coach for offensive line in 2006, with the team continuously since 1982
182. Phil Bengtson, coached five games in 1972
183. Bucko Kilroy
184. *Patriots Football Weekly*
185. Adam Vinatieri
186. Baltimore Colts, in 1975
187. Tom Brady, in April 2005

188. 162 attempts
189. Kevin Faulk, 23 yards
190. J. R. Redmond, 6 yards
191. Troy Brown
192. Troy Brown
193. Drew Bledsoe, playing for the Buffalo Bills
194. Tedy Bruschi
195. Rosevelt Colvin
196. Kevin Faulk, 1996–1998
197. Christian Fauria
198. Willie McGinest
199. Josh Miller
200. Adam Vinatieri
201. Nick Kaczur
202. Matt Cassel, in *Freshman Year*
203. Mike Holovak, hired as director of player personnel in 1959

CELTICS ANSWERS

1. Chuck Connors
2. Frank Ramsey
3. Gene Conley, for baseball with the Milwaukee Braves in 1957 and for basketball with the Celtics in 1959, 1960, and 1961
4. Bill Russell, in 1972
5. Bob Cousy, in 1956–57
6. John Havlicek, in 1974. The award began in 1969.
7. Chuck Cooper, from Duquesne University
8. Bill Russell, in 1979
9. His microphone
10. Rick Pitino
11. Chuck Connors, who starred as *"The Rifleman"*
12. Danny Ainge, in 1981–82
13. Pete Maravich
14. Entering 2006-07, no Celtic has done so.
15. Bob Cousy's
16. Larry Bird, in 1986
17. Henry Finkel
18. Paul Westphal
19. On November 3, 1995
20. Chris Ford, also the first in NBA history
21. Mel Counts, in 1964–65
22. John "Honey" Russell
23. John Havlicek and Larry Bird
24. Their first 100-point game. They beat St. Louis 102-83.
25. Paul Pierce, 2,144 total points in 2001–02
26. 1954–55

27. 60 games, with a record of 60-20
28. Minneapolis Lakers
29. John Havlicek
30. Bill Russell. Between 1958 and 1965, he won the award five times in all.
31. Bob Cousy, 1953–1960
32. Frank Ramsey
33. Bill Russell, from the University of San Francisco
34. Bill Sharman
35. Bill Russell, in 1958, 1960, and 1962
36. Don Chaney
37. Bill Russell, from the University of San Francisco to the Celtics
38. Bill Russell and KC Jones
39. Bob Cousy and Ed Macauley
40. Pete Maravich, at LSU
41. Bill Sharman
42. Paul Westphal
43. Bill and Luke Walton
44. Gary Payton
45. Larry Bird
46. KC Jones, at the Los Angeles Rams camp in 1958
47. Bob Cousy
48. Ruppert Knickerbocker Beer owned the Celtics from 1965 to 1967
49. Connie and Johnny Simmons, in 1946–47
50. Bill Sharman was a late-season call-up for the Brooklyn Dodgers in September 1951. He never got in a game, but he was ejected with the entire bench during a game at Braves Field.
51. Los Angeles Lakers
52. Bob McAdoo. Then-owner John Y. Brown's wife, Phyllis George, suggested McAdoo be acquired.
53. Kevin McHale, in 1981
54. Togo Palazzi, star at Holy Cross, sold to Syracuse
55. JoJo White in 1969–70, Dave Cowens in 1970–71, Larry Bird in 1979–80, and Kevin McHale in 1980–81
56. Chuck Connors
57. Bill Green, in 1963, from Colorado State
58. Tom "Satch" Sanders, in 1978–79
59. Houston Rockets
60. Tom Thacker
61. Jim Loscutoff, known as "Loscy"
62. Dave Cowens
63. Gerry Ward, in 1964–65
64. Winning a sixth consecutive championship. They were the first pro team to accomplish this feat in any sport.
65. Ed Macauley

66. Providence, Rhode Island. The Celtics lost to the Providence Steamrollers.
67. Rich Weitzman, 1967–68 season
68. Toronto Huskies, on November 16, 1946. The Celtics won 55-49.
69. Tommy Heinsohn, 1956–57
70. KC Jones, Sam Jones, Willie Naulls, Bill Russell, and Tom Sanders
71. Moe Becker, traded to Pittsburgh during the 1946–47 season
72. Trainer Buddy LeRoux
73. Gene Conley
74. Nate Archibald, for the Kansas City–Omaha Kings in 1972–73
75. Associated Press Male Athlete of the Year
76. Arnold
77. Bill Sharman, Larry Siegfried, and Larry Bird
78. Bob Cousy, who retired in 1970 at age 42
79. Robert Parish
80. The 1960 U.S. Olympic basketball team, which won the gold medal
81. Amateur athlete and professional writer George Plimpton
82. Bill Russell, in 1967–68
83. Bob Cousy, in 1959
84. Larry Bird, in 1985
85. Pete Maravich, playing for LSU
86. Bill Russell began coaching the Celtics in 1966.
87. Red Auerbach
88. Sam Jones, in 1964–65
89. Ed Macauley, in 1960
90. Larry Bird, in 1985
91. Mel Counts
92. John Havlicek
93. Bill Sharman, scored 42 on December 11, 1952
94. Kevin McHale
95. Glenn
96. Bill Sharman
97. Detroit Pistons
98. Bill Russell
99. Larry Bird. Streets in the Indiana towns of West Baden Springs (his birthplace) and French Lick (his childhood home) are each named Larry Bird Avenue.
100. Red Auerbach: the Red Auerbach Trophy for NBA Coach of the Year
101. Kevin McHale in 1983–84 and Bill Walton in 1985–86
102. Bill Russell was MVP for the 1957–58 season, but a second-team All-Star.
103. Dave Bing, playing for Detroit in 1968
104. Cedric Maxwell, in 1978–79 and 1979–80
105. Dana Barros, playing for Seattle in 1992
106. Robert Parish, with 1,611 games, including 1,106 games for the Celtics

107. Ed Macauley
108. Rick Pitino, with Providence and Kentucky before coaching the Celtics, and Louisville after
109. Larry Bird, with 69
110. Pete Maravich, in 1977
111. Red Auerbach, Bill Russell, Tom Heinsohn, Bill Fitch, and KC Jones
112. Tom Heinsohn, NBA Rookie of the Year in 1956–57 and Coach of the Year in 1972–73
113. Bob McAdoo in 1974–75 and Larry Bird in 1983–84
114. Danny Ainge played for baseball's Toronto Blue Jays and basketball's Boston Celtics and Sacramento Kings.
115. Ten
116. Bob McAdoo, for 1974–75 through 1976–77
117. John Havlicek
118. Bob Cousy and Bill Russell
119. Bob Cousy
120. Tom Sanders fouled out 94 times.
121. Dave Cowens, in 1970–71
122. Owner Walter Brown, during the 1964-65 season
123. Red Auerbach
124. Danny Ainge. The others were Dale Ellis and Reggie Miller.
125. Red Auerbach for 1964-65, Tom Heinsohn for 1972-73, and Bill Fitch for 1979-80
126. Bob Cousy. In 1950 Cousy's name was drawn from a hat in the dispersal draft of the Chicago Stags franchise.
127. KC Jones
128. Pete Maravich
129. Larry Bird
130. Bob Cousy was commissioner of the American Soccer League form 1974 to 1979.
131. Bob Cousy, in a 1953 win vs. Syracuse
132. Bill Russell
133. Bill Fitch
134. Cedric Maxwell nicknamed Parish after Chief Bromden in the Ken Kesey novel One Flew Over the Cuckoo's Nest.
135. KC Jones and Tom Sanders released "The Basketball Twist" in 1963.
136. Whitey Ford, Yankees pitcher, and Dick Lynch, Giants defensive back
137. New York Knicks and Golden State (originally Philadelphia) Warriors
138. Bill Russell, Dave Cowens, and Robert Parish
139. JoJo White, played 488

BRUINS ANSWERS

1. Carol Vadnais, with Oakland in 1969
2. Robbie Ftorek, MVP of the World Hockey Association (WHA) in 1977
3. Jerry Toppazzini
4. Ray Bourque
5. John Bucyk
6. Gerry Cheevers, in 1971–72
7. Don Cherry, in 1977–78. The eleven 20-goal scorers were Wayne Cashman, Stan Jonathan, Don Marcotte, Peter McNab, Rick Middleton, Bob Miller, Terry O'Reilly, Brad Park, Jean Ratelle, Bobby Schmautz, and Gregg Sheppard.
8. Paul Coffey, who played most of his career for the Edmonton Oilers
9. Phil Esposito, in 1970–71
10. Armand "Bep" Guidolin, in 1942
11. Doug Keans, in March 1982, vs. Los Angeles Kings
12. Reggie Leach, in 1976 Stanley Cup playoffs, for Philadelphia Flyers
13. Chris Nilan, on March 31, 1991, vs. Hartford
14. Adam Oates, in 1993
15. Terry O'Reilly, in game 4 of the 1988 finals, vs. Edmonton. The Bruins were swept 4–0.
16. Bobby Orr, in 1969–70
17. Jacques Plante, while playing for Montreal Canadiens
18. Art Ross, in 1929–30 when the Bruins had a record of 38-5-1
19. Jim Stewart, on January 10, 1980
20. Rick Tocchet, in 1992–93, playing for Pittsburgh, 109 points, 252 penalty minutes
21. Willie O'Ree, in the 1957–58 season
22. Milt Schmidt

23. Art Ross
24. Lionel Hitchman, in 1928–29
25. Eddie Shore, in 1945
26. Boston's "Kraut Line," composed of Milt Schmidt, Bobby Bauer, and Woody Dumart, in 1939–40
27. Terry Sawchuk
28. "Tiny" Thompson, in the 1935–36 season
29. Bernie Parent
30. Glen Sather
31. Brian Bellows captained the Minnesota North Stars in 1983 when he was 19 years old.
32. Terry O'Reilly, penalized 2,095 minutes with Bruins
33. Bobby Orr, in 1969–70, 125 penalty minutes, 120 points
34. Eddie Shack. In 1966 "Clear the Track, Here Comes Shack" was number one on Toronto charts.
35. Ken Hodge, born in Birmingham, England, June 25, 1944
36. Joe Juneau, with 102 points, in 1992–93. Teemu Selanne was elected Rookie of the Year.
37. Bobby Orr, with the Bruins in 1971
38. Brad Park, in the early 1980s
39. George Owen, in 1929
40. Gerry Cheevers, in 1967–68, with black stitch marks
41. Frank Brimsek, in the 1940s
42. Lionel Hitchman, in the mid-1930s
43. Numbers
44. Adam Oates, in 2001–02, playing for Washington/Philadelphia, broke Gretzky's record of 15 overtime assists.
45. Dit Clapper, 1927–1947
46. Dit Clapper, in 1947
47. Phil Esposito, Ken Hodge, and Wayne Cashman recorded 336 points in 1970–71.
48. Terry O'Reilly, in 1977–78
49. On February 26, 1981, the Bruins and the Minnesota North Stars were penalized a combined 406 minutes.
50. Phil Esposito, 76 goals, and John Bucyk, 51 goals
51. Ron Tugnutt faced 73 shots for a 3-3 tie.
52. Gilles Gilbert, on February 11, 1982, playing for Detroit
53. Craig MacTavish, in 1985
54. Don Gallinger, in 1948
55. Billy Coutu, in April 1927
56. Marty McSorley, in February 2000, for high-sticking Donald Brashear of the Vancouver Canucks
57. Bobby Orr, in January 1970
58. John Ferguson, in 1994-95, playing for the Montreal Canadiens

59. Milt Schmidt, in October 1960
60. Pat Burns, while he was coaching Montreal Canadiens
61. Phil Esposito
62. Johnny Bucyk, in 1975
63. Bill Cowley, in 1940–41
64. Phil Esposito and Bobby Orr
65. Bobby Orr, who won the James Norris Trophy as best defenseman, 1968–1975
66. Eddie Shore
67. Bobby Orr. His ring was taken into space by Canadian astronaut Robert Thirsk on space shuttle *Columbia* in June 1996.
68. Ray Bourque played from 1980 through 2001 before winning the Stanley Cup with the Colorado Avalanche.
69. Mel Hill, in 1939
70. First team to record more than 120 points in the regular season yet lose in the first playoff round (to Montreal)
71. Robbie Ftorek, in 2000, for New Jersey
72. Bobby Orr won the Art Ross, Norris, Hart, and Conn Smythe trophies for the 1969–70 season.
73. Chris Nilan, in 1984, for Montreal
74. Bob Gryp, in 1973–74
75. John Bucyk, Phil Esposito, Ken Hodge, and Bobby Orr were all 100-point scorers.
76. Cy Dennehy, in 1928–29
77. Dave Forbes, in 1973–77
78. John Bucyk, Phil Esposito, and Rick Middleton
79. Lorne John "Gump" Worsley, on October 23, 1966, playing for Montreal
80. Bill Ezinicki
81. Oshawa Generals
82. Jimmy Herberts, in 1924–25
83. Ottawa Senators
84. Carol Vadnais and Don Marcotte, in 1973–74
85. Ralph "Cooney" Weiland, with 73 points in 1929–30
86. Bobby Orr
87. Bobby Orr
88. John Bucyk
89. Chris Oddleifson, on December 30, 1973, vs. California
90. Barry Pederson, in 1981–82
91. "Tiny" Thompson, Frank Brimsek, Jim Henry, and Pete Peeters
92. Ray Bourque, in 1979–80
93. Goalie Frank Brimsek, in 1938–39
94. Cy Dennehy, in 1928–29
95. Eddie Westfall
96. Dallas Smith

97. John Bucyk in 1971, and Ken Hodge in 1971 and 1974
98. Bobby Bauer, in 1939–40, 1940–41, and 1946–47
99. Brian Leetch, playing for the Rangers in the 1993–94 season
100. Bobby Orr, in 1970 and 1972
101. Jim Craig
102. Rick Middleton
103. Dave Forbes, in 1975 for a stick-swinging incident
104. Derek Sanderson, in 1969
105. Kevin Stevens, with the Pittsburgh Penguins in 1991-92
106. Bill Ranford won Stanley Cups with Edmonton in 1988 and 1990, a Canada Cup with Canada in 1991, and a World Championship with Canada in 1994.
107. Jim Schonfield (1983–84) and Ken Linesman (1984–85)
108. Phil Esposito, in 1971
109. Joe Juneau, in 1996, playing with the Washington Capitals. He failed to score.
110. 29
111. Andrew Alberts, Boston College; and Mark Stuart, Colorado College
112. Bill Guerin, in 2001
113. Adam Oates, in 1993
114. Pete Peeters, in 1983
115. Eddie Shore, in 1928
116. Bobby Bauer, in 1940
117. Steve Kasper, in 1982
118. Don Cherry, in 1976
119. Robbie Ftorek
120. Frank Brimsek
121. Terry Sawchuk
122. Jay Miller, in 1987–88
123. Darryl Sittler, in 1976, playing with Toronto Maple Leafs
124. Rick Middleton and Ray Bourque, 1985–1988
125. Ray Bourque, 1988–2000
126. Robbie Ftorek, in the December 27, 1999, issue
127. Willie O'Ree (1957) and Bryan Berard (2002)
128. Frank Brimsek
129. Garnet "Ace" Bailey
130. Eddie Shore
131. Milt Schmidt
132. John Bucyk
133. 6
134. Barry Pederson
135. Vladimir Ruzicka, in 1990–91
136. "Knuckles"
137. Dennis O'Brien played for Minnesota, Colorado, Cleveland, and Boston.

138. Gordie Roberts
139. Patrice Bergeron
140. Joe Thornton, first pick, and Jay Henderson, final pick
141. Bobby Orr had 102 assists in 1970–71.
142. Ray Bourque. His younger brother is Richard Bourque.
143. In the 1970–71 season, they finished 57-14-7.
144. Brad Park, playing with the Rangers and the Bruins in 1975–76. He was traded from New York to Boston during the season.
145. Against "Tiny" Thompson by his brother Paul
146. Tom Johnson, with 57 wins in 1970–71
147. Dit Clapper won Stanley Cups in 1929, 1939, and 1941.
148. Bobby Orr, on April 11, 1971, vs. Montreal
149. Jean Ratelle, traded from New York to Boston in 1975–76, compiled 105 points for the season.
150. Bill Cowley and Phil Esposito
151. Jimmy Herberts in 1924–25, Bobby Orr in 1969–70, Terry O'Reilly in 1977–78, and Joe Thornton in 1999–2000
152. Nick Boynton in 2001–02, and Andrew Raycroft in 2003-04
153. Mike Knuble, vs. Florida Panthers
154. Cam Neely, on October 7, 1995, vs. New York Islanders
155. Orr wore number 5. Number 4 was taken by Montreal's Jean Beliveau.
156. Phil Esposito, who ended with five, and Cam Neely, who ended with three
157. Bobby Orr, Phil Esposito, Barry Pederson, and Cam Neely
158. Glen Murray
159. Ivan Boldirev
160. Eric Weinrich
161. Mariusz Czerkowski
162. Sandy Moger, on October 7, 1995, in a 4-4 tie with NY Islanders
163. Craig Billington beat Hartford Whalers 3-0 on October 28, 1995.
164. Byron Dafoe, born in Sussex, England
165. Originally owned by the Toronto Maple Leafs as a junior in Ontario, Cheevers was drafted by the Bruins in 1965.
166. Ray Bourque
167. Byron Dafoe
168. Don Simmons
169. Bill and Max Quackenbush, in 1950–51
170. Jim Craig in 1980–81 and Cleon Daskalakis from 1984 to 1987
171. Denis Potvin
172. At the Boston Arena. They moved to the new Boston Garden in November 1928.
173. Gerry Cheevers, in the 1969 playoffs
174. Bronco Horvath, in 1959–60
175. Marcel Bonin. At 16 he wrestled the bear for a $1,000 prize from Barnum & Bailey Circus. He played for the Bruins in 1955–56.

176. Boston Madison Square Garden
177. Pat Burns was a police officer in Hull, Quebec, before entering professional hockey.
178. Pat Egan, who played with the Bruins from 1944 to 1949
179. Ken Hodge Jr.
180. Stan Jonathan
181. Fernie Flaman, Stan Jonathan, and Terry O'Reilly
182. Johnny McKenzie. During a celebration of the 1970 Stanley Cup McKenzie poured a beer on Mayor Kevin White's head. Two years later at a similar celebration White returned the favor!
183. Mike Milbury, in a 1973 brawl in the stands during a Bruins vs. Rangers game at Madison Square Garden
184. Mike O'Connell. His father, Tommy, was a quarterback for the Cleveland Browns in the 1950s.
185. Bobby Orr, playing with the Oshawa Generals, and Derek Sanderson, playing with the Niagara Falls Flyers, in a game at the Garden to showcase the Bruins' amateur talent
186. Randy Burridge. When Burridge scored, he would do a fist pump that became known as the "stump pump."
187. Derek Sanderson, *The Derek Sanderson Show*
188. Derek Sanderson, in 1970, in *Loving and Laughing*. Sanderson was on-screen for approximately 90 seconds.
189. Bobby Orr, Carol Vadnais, Ted Green, and Dallas Smith were known as Bob and Carol and Ted and Dallas. The movie was *Bob and Carol and Ted and Alice!*

About the Author

Owen Finnegan has collected more than 400 sports trivia books and particularly likes to keep track of record-setting firsts. A semi-retired civil engineer for the Town of Wellesley and an athlete himself, he once had a pitching tryout with the Pittsburgh Pirates. He lives with his family in Needham, Massachusetts.